Joho! Publishers (Pty) Ltd,
LIPCO Chambers, Village Walk off Link Road,
Parklands 7441

Published in 2008
First edition

© Naka Pillman

All rights reserved.

Creative editing by Stephanie Nieuwoudt
Proofreading by Bronwyn McLennan

Cover design by Joho!
Cover image from iStockphoto
Typesetting by Joho!

Set in 11.5pt Adobe Garamond

Printed by Paarl Print
Oosterlandstraat, Paarl.

ISBN 9780980275469

www.joho.co.za

An African Cameo

NAKA PILLMAN

By the same author

African Portrait: The Life and Sculpture of Joe Vorster
(Johannesburg: Hugh Keartland, 1976).

Laurika Postma: 'n Biografie (Pretoria: De Jager-Haum, 1984).

African Diary: The Day-by-Day Account of an Incredible Adventure (Mississippi: QRP Books, 1990).

Camel Crochet (Sterling, 1990).

Naka Pillman was born in 1919 in Rustenburg and educated at Pretoria High School for Girls. Showing a talent for both music and art, she received private tuition in these subjects, succeeding in her final music exam with honours at the age of sixteen. She enrolled at the Witwatersrand Technical College where she studied art under the acclaimed Elizabeth MacAdam.

As a life member of the South African Archaeological Society, she has travelled extensively, studying art treasures housed in many world-renowned museums throughout Europe, the Middle East and the Far East, as well as the United States and South America.

Naka is known for being an adventurous traveller. In 1963 she took her eleven-year-old daughter on a 6 000 km journey from Cape Town to Cairo. Alone in Afghanistan she wore a chador and followed the Buddhist route through the foothills and valleys of the Hindu Kush mountain range up to the sacred lakes of Bandi Amir to explore the ancient artworks in the cold Bamiyan caves. In Teheran she had an unfortunate misunderstanding with the police and lived through the adventure of spending time in an Iranian jail. There she discovered their use of a woollen zip, which idea she took to Pennsylvania and taught to the Amish.

She is the author of numerous articles published in educational and art magazines, and specialises in the research of unusual art expression. She is a founder member of the Museum of Man and Science. Presently she lives in George.

To Mary Jones of Yazoo City

PREFACE

In the 1970s, through circumstances beyond my control, I had to intercede in an unpleasant affair on behalf of Yoriko, a highly cultured and multi-talented Japanese woman who ended up staying with me for a while.

After her return to her motherland, she invited me to visit her in Japan. It is so rare for the Japanese to invite strangers to stay with them in their homes that I immediately accepted this great honour.

Japanese houses are incredibly small, and a home is sacred. Japanese people also have great respect for each other's privacy. Close friends don't even drop in casually, as is the custom with us. The women meet at the cultural centre where they enjoy tea together and the men meet privately.

While in South Africa, she started telling me a true story that was so devastating that I could not immediately grasp the true extent of what had happened. During my visit to Japan, her English had improved so much that she could flesh out the story. Many years later, I felt compelled to research both the South African and the Japanese side of the story, and started writing down this chain of events.

In South Africa Yoriko and I perfected a mutually acceptable means of communication by quoting directly from our respective dictionaries. She spoke very little English and I spoke no Japanese.

Our conversations were conducted through a smattering of words, simple sentences and the interrogative lifting of an eyebrow or an appealing glance. In this empathetic manner we were able to meld what proved to become a sincere friendship, across cultural taboos and apartheid pitfalls. As her English improved over the years, we began to correspond, and even though she urged me to publish her story, I had to wait for recognisable features and characters in the story to fade with years. Only now after so many years do I feel comfortable enough to share Yoriko's story. The names of the people involved in Yoriko's story have nevertheless been changed to safeguard those who wish to remain anonymous.

I am honoured by and deeply indebted to Yoriko, who has become a celebrated spiritual painter and is happily married to a university professor.

Naka Pillman
2008

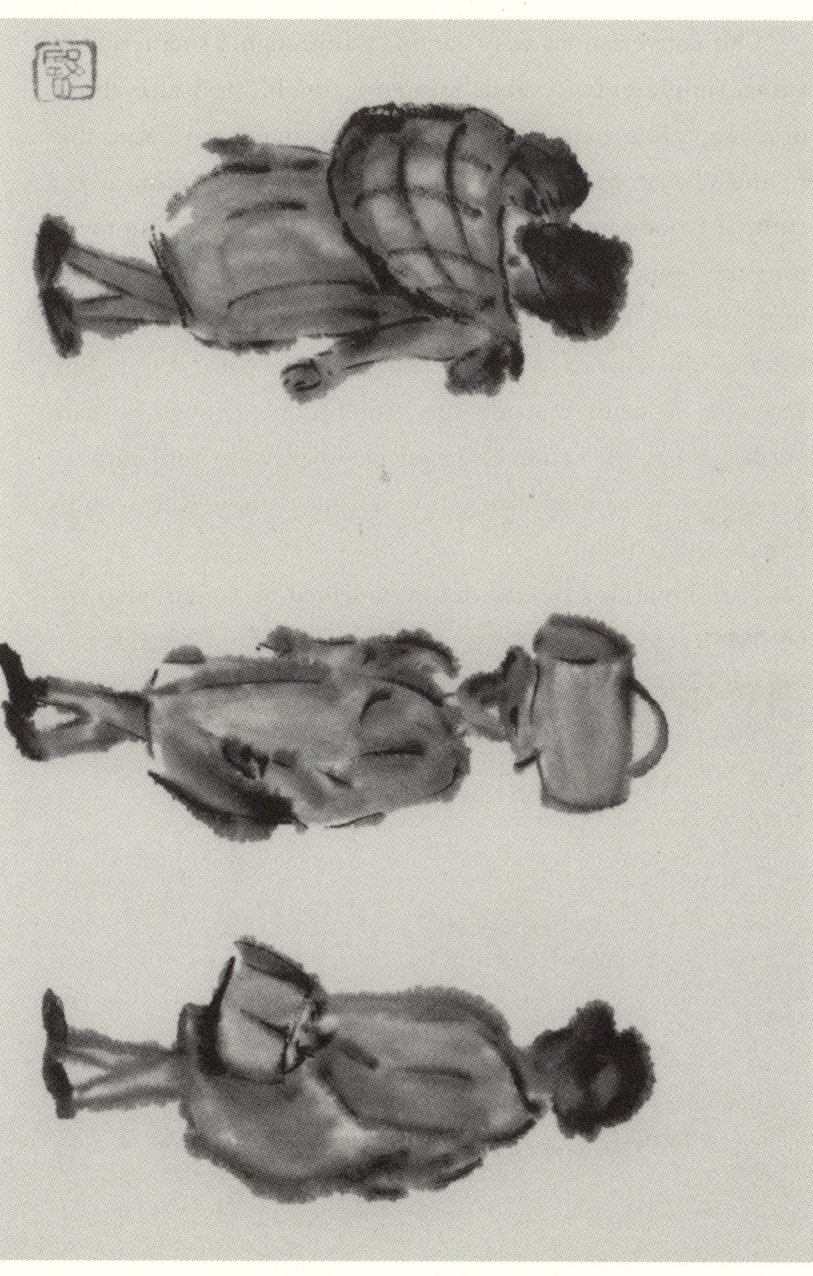

Johannesburg, 1975

The figure on the bed moves slightly. It is a tiny Japanese woman. She groans as the light from the naked bulb overhead pierces her eyes.

She is immediately aware of two things: her body is aching all over and she is naked.

She turns her head slightly and sees the man she loves sitting at a table with a group of black men.

'You're awake, baby,' the man says. 'What fun you had. But now we have to go home.'

He walks closer to her and forces a mug with a foul brew to her lips.

The other men at the table chuckle as Bill Bosch throws a blanket over her before picking her up effortlessly in his arms.

As he walks into the cold night air, Yoriko, with pain shooting up between her legs, loses consciousness for the third time that day.

Tokyo, 1973

We are tourists in Tokyo, discovering the East for the first time. Tony and I are work colleagues: I am an art researcher and Tony an accomplished photographer.

'Look!' he exclaims in delight, focusing my attention on an exquisitely dressed infant girl. She is walking along the street holding the hand of a beautifully dressed woman. They both look like walking dolls, the child a miniature of the mother. We smile at them and they smile back at us.

'May I take a picture?' Tony asks, holding the camera, ready for action. The woman stands still, all the while smiling politely while Tony adjusts the lens of his camera. Both of us are very happy to at long last be in this wonderful country so far away from our homeland, South Africa. We have been eager to make contact with this ancient civilisation of highly cultured people who live in a land of photogenic scenery contrasted with overcrowded cities.

There are priceless works of art everywhere, almost carelessly displayed, as though everybody is conversant with their own ancient and exquisite heritage and accepts these priceless creations as a natural way of life.

Tony points to a sign with the words 'Art Centre'. We wander up the short flight of stairs, stopping often to look at the delicately woven tapestries and wall hangings on display on the side wall next to the stairs.

In the far corner of the showroom we notice a girl in a traditional kimono hovering protectively over a rose quartz vase. She is like an exotic butterfly reflected in the glossy surface of the showcase next to her. When we reach her, she smiles, placing the palms of her small hands together, and bows in the traditional manner of the followers of Buddha.

'I wonder if she can understand English?' Tony muses.

In response the girl smiles. 'Excuse please. I'm sorry no English.' She waves her hand in the air above her head. A young man nods at her from across the room, and walks purposefully towards us.

'May I be of service?' he asks very politely.

'We are just browsing,' I answer. 'This centre is very beautiful.'

'Thank you very much. You are very welcome. We have a fine collection of the very best works of art. Our resident artist is in charge of this department.'

He gestures towards the young girl who is still smiling. 'This is our artist. She has her own government seal. Our government gives this seal only to qualified and registered artists. She may use this seal on all her paintings so that people will know they are paintings of quality! She knows all our famous masters, and if there is anything you wish to ask she will explain it all. I will translate, of course.' He smiles proudly after his introduction, puts his hands together and bows his head to the girl.

'Perhaps she can show us some of her work,' I suggest.

He nods and says something to her in Japanese. The young woman hurries away and while we wait for her to return, I marvel at the beauty which surrounds me. The subtle wash of colour, the impeccably mannered people, their fine clothes, the beauty of their art.

Since arriving in this overcrowded city I have not been able to sleep. To my sensitive ears it sounds as though each of the citizens is standing outside my bedroom window talking.

This morning as we walked along, we could not help gaping at the incredible number of people and cars on roads that seemed much too narrow for dual traffic lanes. Our progress is interesting but slow with Tony busily taking pictures and me staring at the people in their Asian diversity.

We wandered along, happy to follow our noses while feasting our eyes. And this is how we arrived at the cultural centre.

I collect my thoughts and look around me. I hear the man telling Tony that the young woman will give the two of us a demonstration of her painting skills. Tony delightedly prepares his camera and the girl stands quietly while the man steps forward and introduces her to us quite formally.

'Yoriko.' He pronounces her name slowly, and waits for us to repeat it. 'Yoriko.' She smiles and bows. She walks to the table, takes out her paints and arranges a piece of rice paper on an absorbent cloth. She places her paperweights where she wants them, then selects a small soft sable-hair brush. Delicately and with utter control she paints the small branches of a bamboo tree. Then she becomes bolder, takes another sheet of rice paper, and paints a cherry branch with pink buds and full-blown blossoms. Very deft, very professional, and very sure of her ability.

I am enthralled. I take out my notebook and start making notes. We ask many questions, being an appreciative audience and enjoying the opportunity to communicate with this delicate and reserved Japanese lady. When she speaks, it is in Japanese, and the interpreter translates what she says.

Eventually he tells us she wants to know why we are so interested in her paintings. I jump at the opportunity to explain my own interest in art and begin to ask her detailed questions about Japanese art. Realising that I can go on indefinitely, Tony eventually interrupts, saying that we have to get going.

When I tell her that sumi-e art is an unknown form of art in my country, she asks if we know any of the famous artists living in Johannesburg.

Tony and I reply simultaneously that we know the names of all the artists at home. Some of them are personal friends.

'She wants to know if you have heard of Bill Bosch,' the

interpreter asks us. Our smiles congeal as we both realise that we have never heard of him. We ask Yoriko to write down the name. She selects one of her visiting cards and, very carefully, writes the name in capital letters on the back of the card. Her dark eyes search our faces for acknowledgement, though her face remains calm. With well-chosen words we explain to her, through the interpreter, that it is unfortunately quite impossible to know all our artists as our country is so large, and the cities so far apart. Even though we think we know all the artists, there must of course be many we do not know. We apologise.

The interpreter replies: 'She says you know the names of our famous artists, like Sesshu, who is known across the world. Bill Bosch is just as famous as he.'

It is a disconcerting statement. I turn the card over, and notice that the woman's name is printed on it as well as the name of the cultural centre. I put the card into my handbag, promising to enquire about the artist as soon as I get home and to write to her the moment I find him.

'Do you have a message for him?' I ask.

I sense that she doubts our credentials and I become expansive and voluble, even going so far as to ask the interpreter to tell her that I have an art degree, that Tony holds a few gold medals for portraiture and submits work to various publications all over the world. I feel my face getting red, my composure ruffles, and silently I ask myself, 'Why this urge to justify ourselves?' I gather myself, but still persist in pursuing the matter.

Impulsively, and forgetting for the moment that I am in the East and that the people here are more reserved, I grab her arm. 'Of course!' I say. 'He could be an artist from one of our German communities. There are many of them that I do not know. When I get home I will make sure that I get acquainted with his work.'

Her eyes shimmer like silver silk. She is electrified and I am amazed by the sudden change in her.

She scurries away and returns with an envelope with her name on it. The stamp in the corner is a picture of a South African protea. There is no doubt that this letter was posted in Johannesburg, the city in which I live. She invites me to open the letter and read it. I hesitatingly unfold the paper. There is just one page. The address given is a box number at the city's main post office.

I read:

My Dearest Yoriko,

Your letter has arrived. That exquisite gem of literature. It is as much an artistic triumph as the painting you made for me which is hanging on the wall in my room, and to which I lift my eyes each day, in silent and solemn confirmation of our love.

I felt, and still feel, a strange spiritual uplifting after reading it. I am glad to know that this love of yours has brought out a fineness in you which generates true happiness in those around you. My arms are aching to hold you again, my lips to tell you I love you, and my whole body to worship you. And while these wishes live in my soul, time is but a speck in eternity.

As you live in my heart,
Sayonara!
Bill Bosch

'Oh, what a wonderful letter!' I exclaim. Stars shine in her eyes. She presses her small hands together in appreciation, bows her head, and offers melodious words of thanks. Taking one of my own visiting cards from my bag, I hand it to her, saying, 'If ever you are in our country, please contact me. Meanwhile, I will do my best to find your friend.' She looks at the name on the card I have given her. 'Naka!' she exclaims with a happy smile. 'Japanese?' she enquires.

I nod my head. I know what she means. We had hardly been a minute on the street when I had seen my name replicated in large print on many shop fronts in Tokyo. This had intrigued me, as my name is not that well known in my own country.

'Good Samurai name!' Yoriko says, nodding her head and smiling sweetly. We bow to each other and part on the best of terms.

'Did you notice the girl's smile?' Tony asks as we walk away. 'I have never seen a smile quite so patently angelic. That really was a sensitive letter. She must be very much in love with this man if a letter from her elicits such a response from him.'

We walk along in silence. I know that I will never forget this girl.

After a very productive tour, during which I attend classes in sumi-e painting and enrich my life through contact with the exquisite and centuries-old culture of the Japanese, we arrive home.

I immediately start making enquiries about Bill Bosch. Not one of the art galleries or people in my circle of artistic friends and acquaintances have ever heard of him. I look through all the telephone directories of Johannesburg and surrounding areas, but I can find no name to match the one Yoriko had given me. Time passes rapidly and I become engrossed in my art research projects. Thoughts of Yoriko are eventually pushed to the back of my mind.

Tokyo, 1972

Bill presses his forehead against the convex of the Boeing window, craning his neck to get a better view while the plane veers in over Tokyo on its final approach to Narita airport. The tall buildings of the city loom dangerously close as he looks down.

For a moment he experiences fear as the plane appears to drop down into the concrete canyons, but this feeling is instantly replaced by a vivid sensual recall. He closes his eyes and thinks of the Asian prostitutes in the book he has hidden behind the geyser in the bathroom of his flat in Johannesburg. The flat where Dolly, his mistress, lives with their daughter, Ellen.

He always goes back to the pictures of these girls. He has looked at them a million times. The erotic, full-colour images are seared into nerve and tissue by constant scrutinising and fantasy. Now these visual memories culminate in an acute awareness of the real-life pleasures awaiting him as promised in the travel brochure highlighting the twin tourist delights of Hong Kong and Japan.

A satisfied smile plays around his mouth as he catches a glimpse of his reflection in the glass. He has come a long way since his childhood days in a road construction camp in the drought-stricken bushveld of the Transvaal.

The language of his youth was Afrikaans. His mother's family were born and bred in Potchefstroom, a rural town in Western Transvaal, and his father, Bossie, was born in South West Africa to German settlers who later moved to South Africa.

With his heavy accent, Bill's grandfather Heinrich Bosch spoke in a mixture of German and Afrikaans. As a child, Bill loved visiting his Bosch grandparents as they lived in the beautiful mountainous region of Fouriesburg where he could go hunting rabbits in the veld. Grandfather Bosch never had much to say to anybody, but Bill sometimes heard him make disparaging remarks about people to his grandmother. The Afrikaners, the blacks, the English, the Portuguese – he had nothing good to say about anybody.

'The trouble with the people in this country,' Oupa Bosch would say, 'is that they are too lazy to do a stitch of work, and not one of them has ever taken the trouble to learn a proper trade. They would rather sit around and see natives do the work, and then blame them for not doing it right.'

He would steal a roguish glance in the direction of his grandson, whom everybody called Kleinbaas, put his arm around the boy's shoulder and tell him not to forget that he had German blood flowing in his veins and that this was something to be proud of.

'But if you really wanted to use your head, you should

learn to speak English, because the English know how to butter their bread on both sides.'

Although he did not always know what his grandfather Bosch meant when he spoke, Kleinbaas had decided for himself early on in life that he wanted to be rich one day. He had long since seen that the richest people he knew of were all English. The newspapers were printed in English, and if you wanted to buy anything in a shop, you had to speak English to the assistants.

Bill had taken his grandfather's advice to heart. He was proud to say that he considered himself an English South African, married to a true-blue English lady. Mable was his trophy wife, as she was born in England and gave him entrance to the English circles of Johannesburg.

Tokyo, 1955

'Yoriko!'

The child being called is three-year-old Yoriko. She is a tiny girl with luminous eyes and a pale face with flawless skin framed by raven black hair cut in a straight line. But even at this tender age her education in the disciplined ways of the well-bred ladies of Japan is already firmly established.

It is 3 March, the day on which the annual Hina Matsuri (Festival of the Dolls or Girl's Day) is held. Ceremonial dolls resembling ancient emperors and empresses and their retinues are brought out for display and prayers are said to ensure the future happiness of the girl children in the family. Respect is shown to ancestors who have passed on.

Traditionally, the first day of spring is also celebrated on this day in what is known as the Peach Blossom Festival.

For the first time, Yoriko is going to visit the family shrine, where she will worship her ancestors with her mother, Noriko, her grandmother, Keiko, her aunt Kato and Tsjisji, who is both maid and companion to the women.

It is a solemn occasion, and Yoriko has been cautioned to behave. In Japan, no child cries in public. At her age Yoriko is no longer regarded as a small child.

It is a class conscious society, and since her infant days it has been impressed on Yoriko that her family is high-class. As befits a child of her family's standing, it is expected of her to be submissive to her elders.

As the little girl enters the room with a sidelong glance at the family group, she is fully aware of their admiration. She is an adored, beautiful daughter who has learnt from experience that the women of the family do not always need words to speak. A fierce glance of their almond-shaped eyes can rein her in if she steps out of line, and a raised eyebrow asks a number of questions. This mannerism expresses the meaning, mystery and intrigue that lie hidden behind a calm countenance.

Despite being so young, Yoriko is wearing a splendid traditional red silk kimono. The other women are equally beautifully dressed in kimonos made from the finest silk. At the shrine the women will pray for the spiritual happiness of Yoriko's father, who died when she was only four months old. Yoriko lowers her gaze in the way she has noticed her elders do, and then opens her eyes in a most beguiling manner, looking from one family member to the other.

Yoriko's father, Isamu, was a doctor. But national overcrowding and insufficient family funds had prevented him from buying his own house when he married. He took his young bride, Noriko, to his paternal home and she moved into the house in which he had grown up.

However, the house was small and the young couple was

forced to move into the room previously occupied by the maid, Tsjisji, next to the kitchen. Tsjisji had to roll out her tatami mat in a small space in the living room at night.

With the unexpected death of Isamu two years before, Noriko and her young daughter had moved into the main bedroom with the older woman in order for the grandmother to help with the child. The grandmother, Keiko, doted on the little girl. Between them, the three women guided Yoriko in the customs and traditions of the highclass. Her aunt, Kato, who lived nearby, visited regularly, and also played a huge part in Yoriko's formative years.

Tokyo, 1957
The air is crisp outside. The many birds chirping in the trees herald the arrival of warmer weather. As the group of women walk along the grassy slope surrounding the temple garden, they take care to step only on the smooth flat stones laid conveniently close together for their dainty feet to reach easily.

Yoriko glances from tree to tree, pointing out the first pink buds opening into their summer splendour. She enjoys the movement of the leaves fluttering in the breeze, as there is no space for a garden outside their own home.

The gate to their house in the Fourteenth Chome opens directly from the street onto a small porch in front of the house where there is just enough room for a shoe stand – made of slats of wood – onto which they place their street shoes before entering.

Perhaps anticipating her granddaughter's affinity for nature, Keiko bought Yoriko a fifty-year-old bonsai cedar tree when she was born. Keiko left the tree in the capable hands of the gardener until today. It is Yoriko's fifth birthday and the tree will be handed over to her with a beautiful ceremony.

The miniature tree is a symbol that she is considered old enough to be given some responsibility. Keiko gently guides her granddaughter in the age-old art of caring for bonsai. She is satisfied when the girl assumes her duty with the same discipline she shows in other aspects of her life. Every morning, after waking up, she treads lightly across the tatami mats that cover the floor of the bedroom and slips quietly out of the house onto the tiny front porch where her grandmother has placed the tree amongst a few rocks next to the front door.

She holds the watering can with both hands and carefully pours a few drops of water onto the moss covering the roots of her tree. Each day she counts the spiky needles forming in bunches at the ends of the tiny branches. This daily commitment is a game as well as a discipline, and Yoriko does not fail in her duty.

One day, after she has been tending the tree for a few months, she calls her mother excitedly. With sparkling eyes, she shows the woman the new buds nestling like little brown buttons in the centre of the cluster of pine needles. They watch them grow over a number of weeks, noticing how they elongate into candle-shaped cones. In the same way, the women watch Yoriko grow and fuss over her, noticing how she is getting prettier and more elegant as the years go by.

Tokyo, 1964

At twelve Yoriko is fine-limbed, delicately proportioned, and graceful.

Her mother instills in her the essential feminine accomplishments required of every well-born Japanese girl; she learns to control her facial expression, to smile and reflect only her willingness to please.

The gentle pattern of Yoriko's life is greatly disturbed when her beloved grandmother dies. Tsjisji teaches her to be thankful that she has many close family ancestors on the other side of the grave, directing her life and giving her spiritual guidance. Yoriko resolves to be strong and self-reliant. She makes a secret vow that she will do nothing to disappoint the ancestors, and do her utmost to uphold the trust they have placed in her.

In spite of her valiant efforts, Noriko, now the head of the family, is unable to afford the upkeep of the house. She is forced to take up residence in an infirmary for the aged.

It is decided that Tsjisji must leave for the countryside to work in a house where young girls learn the ancient art and traditions of the geisha. With many tears and many bows of heads, Tsjisji eventually departs. Yoriko is sent to stay with her aunt Kato, who owns a very small two-bedroomed house. The second tiny bedroom is let to a teacher.

Having no children of her own, Kato has the means to lavish all her love and attention on Yoriko. More importantly, she will help Yoriko to prepare for a marriage suited to her social status.

A good marriage is the ultimate dream of every parent for their daughter, and to prepare her for this role in life, a Japanese girl must be obedient and radiate an inner charm and happiness. The first step is to attract an eligible husband from whom the whole family may benefit. The next step is for both sides of the family to enter into negotiations about a marriage.

Each day after school, Kato shows Yoriko how to clean the small area where the teacher lives and sleeps. The young girl has to go down onto her knees, carefully sweeping the floor with a soft hand brush. Sometimes the teacher arrives home when she has not quite finished. He stands a few paces away, waiting patiently for her to complete her task, and then walks into the room while Yoriko remains seated on her heels with palms pressed together and head bowed courteously. She does not lift her head, nor does she gaze up at him, but waits for her aunt, whom she knows will appear almost instantly to brew his tea in the traditional ceremonial manner. She, the pupil, will be expected to assist her in this ritual.

While the teacher and Kato speak, Yoriko waits patiently, sometimes listening, though not always understanding what is being said. At night Yoriko kneels in front of the shrine in the corner of the living room and prays, repeating the words she has learnt from Kato and her mother, Noriko.

'Dear spirits of my illustrious ancestors! Give me a strong heart like a samurai. May my spirit reflect the glory of my ancestors like the rays of the sun sparkling from the summit of Mount Fuji!'

Tokyo, 1966

Yoriko's life continues happily. She studies, helps her aunt to keep the house clean and learns the intricacies of the tea ceremony.

When the lodger teacher asks her a question, she replies with a youthful animation which brings a smile to the eyes of the tired old man. She is beautiful, and Kato entertains the idea of sending her to Tsjisji so that she may learn the profession of the geisha. For a girl who is almost an orphan, with only a modest dowry, the option of becoming the geisha mistress of a rich man is a worthy and honourable one. Yoriko patiently listens to her aunt speculating about the wonderful and secure alternative life a girl with her beauty and grace can have as a geisha, should a marriage proposal not be forthcoming. But, although she does not say anything, Yoriko has been nurturing other ideas about her future.

She has always felt a compulsion to reproduce that which moves her. It comes naturally to her to use a brush and ink to draw on silk or paper whatever she sees. She does not know how to tell her family that she wants to become a sumi-e artist who, with only a few strokes of a brush, can capture the very core of whatever is being painted.

She cannot imagine a life doing anything else. The thought of marrying and subjecting herself to a husband's wishes is something she cannot contemplate now. She knows her family will be shocked to learn that she does not want to become that for which she has been groomed from birth.

At school she continues with her work diligently and when she is chosen to attend special classes in flower arrangement at the cultural centre, she is overjoyed. She becomes a dedicated Ikebana pupil, experiencing an almost sensual pleasure in the perfect beauty of the triangular flower arrangements she makes. Each bloom is arranged according to its yin and yang response to the contrasting vibrations of the earth. To become a master Ikebana artist can take up to forty years. It is a journey in which one learns to arrange each flower, plum and bamboo shoot at exactly the right time and in exactly the right order. Certain plant materials simply cannot be used together, as this will anger the ancestors and bring bad luck.

After her Ikebana classes, she rushes to her desk to reproduce these arrangements as sumi-e paintings. In the tradition of the true sumi-e artist, she pours her heart and soul into the paintings. In this way, she is not merely an artist. She becomes her subject.

Yoriko is a multi-talented child who is frequently the topic of discussion during teachers' meetings. It does not happen often that one teacher commends a pupil to a teacher of another class. However, this privilege befalls Yoriko, who is given an honourable discharge from the Ikebana class and transferred to the sumi-e teacher.

Yoriko is elated. She is convinced that this is the answer to her secret prayers. Surely this is a sign that she will one day become a revered artist. She applies herself passionately to her studies in this ancient art form.

For the first few weeks her right arm aches from constantly curving her fingers around an invisible egg that she has to imagine pressing into the palm of her hand while holding the paint brush lightly but firmly upright, as is required of the sumi-e artist. She welcomes the physical pain. It is a manifestation that she is on the path to fulfil her dream. The desire to be creative is overwhelming. It consumes her. For her, the ultimate happiness would be isolation so that she could paint without interruption. She finds pleasure in the discipline of memorising the exact shape and growth pattern of every flower she comes across. All famous sumi-e painters recommend this daily memorisation technique.

Each day she prays to her ancestors that she may be accepted and recognised as an artist of merit.

Tokyo, 1968

When the family members meet, they talk at great length about Yoriko, The Clever One, who has been favoured by the ancestors. She is sixteen years old and her accomplishments in Ikebana and sumi-e painting have enhanced her prospects of marriage. The family has already received messages from a number of families declaring their intentions to negotiate. The older women stress the economic need for one specific eligible and influential young man to be accepted, and for a wedding date to be agreed upon as soon as possible.

When she is informed that her family has identified a suitor and that they plan on entering into discussions with his family, Yoriko is devastated. She cannot wait any longer. She has to confront her family.

A meeting attended by all the family members is held to discuss how the negotiations should be arranged. The older people take turns congratulating Yoriko on her good fortune. When it is time for Yoriko to speak, her gaze is timid and her hands tremble in a gesture of supplication. In a plaintive voice she puts her case forward.

'Please, Yoriko begs forgiveness! I, who have no rights to ask any favours, I beg you to allow me to speak. I wish to make known the innermost wishes of my heart!' She bows her head. 'The creative urge of my spirit has taken over my life.'

Kato answers her: 'Becoming a master in the ancient art of sumi-e painting is founded on a life dedicated to Zen. Only men excel in this art form. True artists are philosophers, schooled in the art of life, who explore their innermost thoughts in peace. They have always been men who have no time or energy to squander on such irrelevancies as food and clothing. They depend on intelligent, understanding wives to support them.'

Kato tells the other family members that the teachers have indeed been lavish in their praise of Yoriko's abilities as an artist, but it has been bestowed on no more than childish endeavour and diligent application. She is talented, but it is a talent that will enhance her standing as a wife.

The family group glances at Yoriko while they exchange more opinions. They are proud of the matrimonial future of this clever young member of their family.

But Yoriko does not give in. She speaks up, telling her family that she cannot become involved in this marriage. She needs more time to soar. To explore her creativity.

Hastily Yoriko is sent to the confines of her tatami mat, where she tries in vain to sleep while the family members converse until late into the night. Another family conference is arranged and a date is agreed on which they will all proceed to the family shrine. There they will contact a priest whom they will pay to pray to their ancestors. The ancestors will give them the answers through the priest.

A few days later, the Buddhist priest welcomes them solemnly. He listens carefully to what each member has to say. He sends them home with the promise that he will seek answers. They have to return within a few days when, he assures them, there will be more clarity.

Yoriko is nervous as she counts off the days before the meeting with the priest. When they meet again, he tells them that in the distant past there was a member of their clan who was a painter. He was Oyo, The Positive One, a genius of great antiquity. But Oyo did not achieve fame. The priest is convinced that the painter's restless spirit will find everlasting happiness should he be called upon to assist in the dreams of a sincere and talented member of their family.

The family has no choice but to accept the words of the priest. After all, the ancestors spoke directly to him. In future, Yoriko has to direct her prayers to Oyo, her ancestral benefactor and omnipotent spiritual entity.

However, Yoriko's mother, Noriko, is unsatisfied with the outcome. She is not convinced that Yoriko's future lies in the solitary life of an artist. She arranges a visit to a famous fortune-teller with her sister Kato and Yoriko.

On the day of the visit, the women take great care to dress

appropriately for the occasion. They do not wear their very best clothes, in case the fortune-teller thinks that they are poor people pretending to be rich. Nor do they wear their shabby old clothes, in case it gives the impression that they are rich people trying to avail themselves of benefits to which they are not entitled.

Kneeling on the floor with her hands on her knees, Yoriko sits back on her heels. The fortune-teller looks at her intently, then closes his eyes. Her aunt and mother are sitting right behind her. She hears him talking as if from a great distance.

'The future is dominated by the heartache of the present. There is a man in the distance, looking in this direction. He is a member of a successful, high-class family. There is also a moth flying towards a flame. It seems as if the man has observed life through this flame for many years. It burns brightly and strongly, and he holds his hands towards the flame, moving them as though he would catch the moth in the palms of his hands.'

Yoriko darts a startled glance at her mother and aunt, but the fortune-teller continues.

'The future is shrouded in a cloud, and through this cloud there shines a very bright light. Success will be in this light, but the cloud will first become even darker, growing as large as a whole continent. But truth will eventually bring light. The message of the future is based on truth.'

When she lies in bed at night, Yoriko replays the words of the fortune-teller in her head. He had said that truth would be the guiding light in her life. But there is nothing simple about the dictates of tradition and the differing opinions of her family; truth gives not one straightforward answer.

South Africa, 1933

Bettie Bosch screws up her eyes to view the flintstone koppies on the horizon. It is only nine o'clock in the morning, but already the monotonous screeching of the cicadas is causing a ringing in her ears, blocking out any possibility of constructive thought. This heat is unbearable and she does not know how to keep her baby son, Kleinbaas, cool. She smiles as she looks at this boy whom the labourers call Kleinbaas, the small son of the big Baas.

She and her husband Bossie married young, and planned to have many children, but they had to wait four years before this baby was born. She sometimes feels a tug of heartache when she recalls what the doctor had said about her and Bossie having more children.

She was heavily pregnant with Hendrik and visiting her parents in Potchefstroom when the first labour pains started. They rushed her to hospital, where little Hendrik was born, blue in the face and struggling to breathe. The tiny body was swollen and he was ill with jaundice. The doctor told them that Bossie's blood and her blood were incompatible.

Everyone feared that Kleinbaas was going to die. Bettie could not bear the thought that she would have to bury her child. With grim determination she decided that he had to live. She prayed fervently and would not leave his side until the baby eventually became better. The doctor told her it was a miracle, but he warned her not to have any more children.

Bettie's mother, Tant Elsie, insisted that Bettie and the baby stay with them for a while until the infant was stronger. During the week, Bossie went back to his work at the road camp, and on weekends he would ride his bicycle to Potchefstroom to visit them.

A few months after the birth, he arrived in Potchefstroom with a handcart and two oxen. He had come to fetch his wife and baby.

She smiles at the fat, eight-month-old baby, caressing his bare shoulder where he sits on the camp stretcher in his nappy. His skin is tanned nut-brown from being exposed to the hot September sun. She will not let him stay in the sun too long today. The sand is already scorching hot.

This drought is the worst of the century so far. When she woke up this morning, she looked up at the sky, hoping for just one little cloud to bring a promise of rain.

When it rains, the river fills up and she sits under a willow tree on the riverbank watching over her baby and listening to the flow of the water. The wives of the Sotho road workers come here regularly to wash their clothes, singing their rhythmic harmonies while beating their wet washing on the rocks. Listening to theirs voices is one of the few pleasures of living in the veld. It is a lonely life being the only white woman in the camp.

Growing up, people often commented on the likeness between Bettie and her mother, Tant Elsie: both were blonde, well-built and soft spoken. At sixteen, Bettie was the youngest and only daughter in a family of five brothers. Her brothers had all married and moved to the Witwatersrand, where they worked at various jobs in the gold mines.

Helping her mother to cook traditional vegetable stews was her main occupation during the day. She would spend hours sitting in the shade of a tree at the back of the boarding house where she lived with her parents, helping her mother cut beans and peel potatoes.

She was not a particularly outgoing child, and did not mind being left on her own. She loved it when her father taught her Afrikaans poems, which she recited to the calls and sounds of the wild bird songs. Her family said she was a dreamer, and her father, a retired teacher, thought it his duty to impress on her the basic facts regarding her Afrikaans heritage, history being the subject he'd taught at school.

Named after the late president, Stephanus Johannes Paulus Kruger, Bettie's father was slightly built with a rather dark complexion. A dedicated educator, he believed that teaching was a sacred profession and, indeed, school teachers like her father were highly respected by the community. He was adamant that he received his calling from God, and nobody ever disputed this sentiment. The Christian schools had been started by the Afrikaners with the aim of consolidating Afrikaners into a nation with Christian values bound together by one language: Afrikaans.

Over the years, Bettie's father had sharpened his natural wit to a satirical pitch with his critical surveillance of his fellow men, and more especially the Afrikaners, whom he held responsible for losing the Boer War against the British.

Many times he would put his arm around her shoulder and say: 'You know what the trouble is with us? We don't know who we are. We don't even know if we are sheep or goats. What we need is forty years in the desert to get to know ourselves, and for that we need a Moses. But even then, we will argue and say, "Moses is a Jew and we are Calvinists!" Who will lead us into the desert where we can come to our senses? God only knows! For that we will need a miracle!'

Her father thought sixteen children were ideal for a good-sized Afrikaans family. His mother had had as many, and even though most of them had died in a concentration camp, she'd insisted that she would never forget any of them.

Bossie's family also suffered through war. They were still

living in South West Africa when World War I broke out, and Bossie's father, Heinrich, was interned by the British. Bossie would never be able to forget his father's haggard face when he was released after the war.

His mother died during the 1919 flu epidemic – a year after the war. An introvert by nature, Bossie could not reach out to his father, even though, at eight years of age, he was poignantly aware of the harm the internment had inflicted on his father's proud spirit.

A subsequent drought in the area where they were farming had squeezed every drop of lifeblood from the starving animals. Bossie was relieved when his father decided to move to a farm near Fouriesburg in South Africa. Eventually, he set off on a visit to relations in Potchefstroom to look for work.

That was when he met Bettie, and he immediately decided that she was the girl he wanted to marry. The feeling was mutual, and when he asked for her hand, Bettie did not hesitate. Her own parents had married when they were even younger than them, and Bettie had no doubts about her love for Bossie. She was even willing to follow her new husband to the government road camps where foremen were needed. She told him that she was not afraid of living in the veld.

Bossie's father was the only one who had his misgivings about the job. He would have preferred if his son had become an apprentice to a carpenter or other tradesman so that he would be assured of having a skill that could support him and his family for the rest of his life. He himself was a diesel mechanic, and in this capacity he had become a handyman and jack-of-all-trades to the farming community in Fouriesburg.

He was not in favour of the ambition of those Afrikaners who wanted their sons to qualify as white-collar workers. He insisted that as artisans, the Afrikaners could more easily become involved in the planning and the economic and business development of the country, instead of leaving it all to the British.

Despite his father's misgivings, Bossie and his wife eventually moved to the camp. He was paid five shillings a day and two 4-gallon tins of paraffin a month for the hurricane lamps and the Primus stove on which Bettie cooked their meals. They also kept a few chickens that ran free in the veld, but they had to lock them in the tool shed at night to keep the jackals away.

As she watches over her son, Bettie smiles as she thinks of her husband. He is a good man and they are very happy.

Once a month, Bossie rides the twenty miles to Potchefstroom on his bicycle and brings back a few essential groceries, such as mealiemeal, salt, sugar, and coffee, and four live chickens for the next month's Sunday meals. Bettie always looks forward to cooking the Sunday lunch, which consists of yellow rice spiced with turmeric and raisins, and brown beans cooked with sugar and vinegar. The chicken will be baked golden brown in the veld oven, which Bossie fires for her the previous night. For pudding, they always have souskluitjies, those delicious cinnamon dumplings she prepares so well.

During the week they live on mieliepap and boiled pumpkin, or pumpkin fritters. Bossie does not hunt. He does not like killing animals. They only have red meat when Bossie is given some as a present by one of the traders who periodically uses this outspan for grazing oxen on the way to and from the coast.

Bettie and her family live on a small piece of the five morgen of veld that had been fenced off as a regular outspan for ox-wagons using this inland route to a seaport on the East African coast. The landscape has no salient feature to recommend it, except for one large tree, under which the traders usually set up camp.

Bossie pitched his family's tent under a cluster of tall kareebossies in the corner of the camp. Sheets of corrugated iron were used to build a storeroom close by, where the Bosches keep their paraffin rations as well as the shovels and other implements necessary for road work.

The ground around the camp is rocky, barren, dry and unsuitable for cultivation. Growing anything near the river is impossible. The spring hares devour every green sprig as soon as shoots start showing above ground. And besides, during this drought, there is no water for a vegetable garden. Most of the available water is given to the oxen that the road workers use to pull the gravel carts on the roads.

The farmer, Andries Venter, on whose farm this outspan has been fenced off, is a kind man who empathises with the people in the camp. Ons the occasional Sunday he invites Bossie and his family to join him and his wife and sons for an afternoon church service and an evening meal. The Bosch family always accepts the offer gratefully. They know there will be huge slabs of meat roasted on the coals and mieliepap with milk, butter and sugar. Often the farmer's wife sends one of the women working in the kitchen over to the camp with a jug of fresh milk for Kleinbaas.

One morning the milk is brought by a Sotho woman Bettie has not seen before. She carries a small child tied onto her back with a colourful shawl. Kleinbaas is sitting on the grass mat in front of the camp bed, amusing himself by digging his fingers into the fine red sand. The woman hands over the milk and then loosens the shawl, swings the black boy off her back, and puts him down on the ground next to Kleinbaas. The babies look at each other with friendly smiles while Bettie puts the milk into the wire mesh charcoal cooler hanging in the trees. The woman is clearly in no hurry to leave.

Eventually Bettie asks: 'Can I help you?'

The woman lowers her head and answers: 'I need work.'

Bettie watches the black child move closer to Kleinbaas as she tells the woman that there really is no work in this camp.

The woman glances at Bettie and says, 'I can do the washing and ironing.'

As Bettie watches her son and the little black boy, she thinks that it would be a good thing for Kleinbaas to have a playmate now that he is beginning to crawl around everywhere. Maybe it would be good to have this woman and her child in the camp during the day. She has taken an immediate liking to her.

'I will speak to the Baas when he comes home. When you bring the milk tomorrow, I will tell you his decision,' Bettie says.

The woman smiles, picks up her baby and swings him onto her back. Nodding her head in farewell, she walks away briskly.

As soon as Bossie arrives at camp, Bettie tells him about the Sotho woman wanting work. 'Tell her she can work for her food,' he says, 'and a cake of soap for the washing. You must see to it that she washes herself as well. They do not know what it is to use soap. These women plaster mud all over their bodies. They mix it with rancid fat and it smells terrible. My mother never tolerated it in our house.'

The next morning the woman arrives early, greeting Bettie in Sotho. She sits down with her baby on the grass mat in front of the camp bed on which Bettie is sitting with Kleinbaas. Next to the bed is a chest of drawers which Bettie has covered with a small tablecloth. Outside, under the huge marula tree, are four folding chairs and a table, where Bettie serves their meals.

'What is your name?' Bettie asks.

'Boaphelo,' the woman replies without looking at Bettie.

'Is that your surname?' The woman does not answer.

'You mustn't be shy,' Bettie reassures her. 'I have spoken to the Baas, and he says you can work for me. But you must have a Christian name. What is it?'

The woman explains that she does not have a Christian name. 'But you must have one,' Bettie exclaims. 'I think we must call you Anna.'

She leans forward to touch the woman on the shoulder. When she looks up, Bettie accepts this as agreement.

'All right,' Bettie says, giving her shoulder a friendly pat. 'Your name is Anna.'

Bettie lies back against the cushions on the bed while Anna picks up her child and starts to breastfeed him.

'What is your baby's name?' she asks.

'Boy,' Anna replies.

'And how old is Boy?'

Anna holds up three fingers.

'Three!' Bettie exclaims in disbelief.

Anna nods her head, and starts to explain in Afrikaans that Boy was a very small baby.

'His father did not want such a small baby and left me. He said he was going to Johannesburg to work in the mines and get a lot of money.'

'But if Boy is three years old, why do you still breastfeed him? Was he sick when he was born?'

Anna laughs. 'He was sick, but now he is healthy. It is our custom to breastfeed our children for a long time.'

'Where is his father?'

'He is somewhere in Johannesburg. He promised my father he would pay him five cows if I would have his baby and marry him. But when the baby was born and he saw the child was sick, he paid only one cow, and said the baby was too small and he did not want to marry me. When the baby got better, I decided to leave home with him. I walked for months. When I got to this farm, Baas Venter gave me food, but he said I should look for work elsewhere, because he does not have enough work on the farm. I have been looking for work for a long time.'

'I am sorry,' Bettie replies, 'we better fatten him up with solid food. He is too old to drink from your breast.'

Anna shakes her head vigorously. 'As long as I feed him, no man will sleep with me, and the grandmother cannot claim him either.'

'How many children do you have?' Bettie asks, thinking that Anna could not have many children as she seems so young and innocent.

Anna tells Bettie about her other two children, aged eight and five, who are staying with their fathers' people in Lesotho, a tiny country surrounded on all sides by South Africa.

'Why do they stay with their fathers' people and not with you?'

'Because they are paid for; they belong there.' Anna continues: 'His grandmother wants Boy to live with her. But I don't want to give him to her. If I can show him to his father, he will have to keep his word and marry me, pay my father, and make my people happy, because I am a good girl.'

Bettie shakes her head. 'Why did you sleep with all the men?'

Her gaze fixed on the ground, Anna answers. 'If a man

wants to play with you, you cannot say no, because you are a woman. When a baby is born, he can say it is not his baby, and your mother can keep the baby, because you are a bad girl. When a baby is born, the man who played with the girl has to pay damages to the girl's father. If the man's mother wants the child, you give it to her, because the child belongs to the man's family if he is paid for.'

'Damages?' Bettie asks in amazement.

'Yes,' Anna explains. 'If a girl is good she can fetch a high bride price or lobola, as we call it. My price was eleven cows. When the first baby arrived, I was still very young and did not want to get married to that man. He only paid one cow for damages to my father. His mother took the baby. After that, the lobola was reduced to ten cows. Then the second baby arrived, and this man also did not want to get married, but he did not have a cow for paying the damages, so he paid my father in money, and his people took the child. Then I met Boy's father and he said he wanted to marry me, because I have pretty children. He wanted a big, strong baby. A wedding was arranged, and he promised to pay, but when this small baby arrived he changed his mind and disappeared. He is a nice man, and I would like to marry him. Yes, I want this one's father,' she says nodding her head in Boy's direction.

Bettie looks at Anna incredulously. Anna says she is a

Christian, and now she tells these stories about the different fathers of her children.

'Aren't you sorry you let all these men make you pregnant?'

Shrugging her shoulders Anna shifts her position on the grass mat. 'You, a white woman, asks me if I am sorry that I slept with all these men. That I was not a virgin when I met the father of this child. But what is a virgin? You tell me you lose it when you allow a boy to play with you. But in our kraal all the girls live and sleep together. It is the custom that girls play with themselves, and the older women teach us from an early age what to expect when a baby is born. A birth is a miracle, and as the girls and boys grow up we play together, practising for that day. Only when your body bleeds for a child, then you tell your mother. The boy who plays with you then knows that he will have to pay your father if you become pregnant.'

Bettie shakes her head in amazement. She too looked forward to the day when she would fall pregnant and give birth to that miracle. But when she grew up, she was told not to touch herself or allow anybody else to touch her private parts because only bad girls did that. The miracle of the consummation of love and the conception of life, she was taught, should only take place after she was married. This would guarantee that her child would be born in the image of

God, and with the blessing of the church and the family.

'Well, what are you going to do now?' Bettie asks Anna.

'I want to work and get money,' she replies.

'But we haven't got money to give you,' says Bettie. 'I told you what the Baas said, that we would give you food and soap and some clothes for you and Boy.'

'I want to live here,' Anna replies.

'But we have no place for you and Boy to sleep.'

Anna nods her head in the direction of the storeroom. 'We can sleep in there.'

'There is no room for you in there,' Bettie says with conviction. Anna heaves a sigh of resignation and gets to her feet.

When she has finished doing the work around the camp, Anna ties Boy onto her back, lifts Kleinbaas onto her hip, and asks Bettie to place the bundle of washing on her head, before she strolls down to the river.

Bettie looks across the veld towards the small hills far away, where red dust swirls relentlessly in perfect spirals across the veld. Bettie has told Anna not to allow Kleinbaas to take off his hat. Aside from the hat he is naked: her son does not like to be restricted by clothes and in this heat it is too hot for clothing, anyway. The child has succeeded in wriggling himself out of his nappy. Well, at least it prevents her from running out of nappies, Bettie smiles to herself. Being poor, she only has two of everything, and has to do the washing every day just to keep things clean. The way the clothes and linen are beaten on the rocks ensures they don't last very long, either. And all the nappies are stained a permanent red-brown from the muddy water, especially now in the dry season.

She sees Anna coming back along the veld path. Kleinbaas has fallen asleep and she has tied him on her back where he rests comfortably against her ample buttocks with his head between her shoulder blades. She walks with a rhythmic stride, swinging her hips and planting each bare foot a good length ahead of the other in a measured tread.

Anna and Boy become a part of the camp life. Anna works hard and Boy and Kleinbaas are firm friends. Kleinbaas speaks Sotho fluently and this is the language in which he and Boy communicate. Bettie sometimes has difficulty understanding what her son is trying to say as he switches between Afrikaans and Sotho, and she has to reprimand him to speak Afrikaans.

On her days off, Anna usually goes for a walk in the veld, looking for wild fruit, and sometimes if Kleinbaas cries she takes him along. She is happy working for Bettie, and as time passes they establish a bond of mutual respect and trust. Together they nurse the boys through childhood ailments and accidents. As the road camp is miles away from the mud huts of the natives living on Venter's farm, the boys have nobody else to play with, and become inseparable.

During the heat of the afternoons, after Anna has finished her chores and the babies are playing happily together under the trees, Bettie invites Anna into the tent and asks her to tell her more about her childhood.

'I come from beyond the mountains of Lesotho,' Anna tells her. 'This is where my father's people live, and the father of this child as well.' She turns to look in the direction of Boy. 'It is good cattle country with good grazing. Sometimes there is snow on the tops of the high mountains. There is plenty of water, and it is a beautiful place to live.'

Anna peers into the distance visualising the scene. She tells Bettie how the older women of her tribe take the girls for walks into the veld, pointing out to them which roots, leaves, and fruit they can eat, and teaching them the traditional songs of the tribe along the way.

She also tells Bettie about the days when women, children and even men in Africa were not safe. In the days of the slave trade, the chiefs who sold women would catch them while they were walking along the footpaths, tie them together and march them to the river where the slave traders were waiting. Sometimes they would force the women onto rickety boats and take them down the river or march them through the bush for days on end. Some of the traders were white men from across the sea who would take the women to far away countries. Others were from Africa and would sell the women to other tribes.

Bettie finds Anna's stories about her people fascinating. She mulls them over during the long and lonely weekends when Bossie has to go to Potchefstroom to buy their supplies for the month.

The next time Bettie, Bossie and Kleinbaas visit her parents in Potchefstroom, Bettie tells Anna's story to her father. Assured of his ability to supply answers to life's questions, she listens while he tells her of the hundreds of years during which the black people of Africa were submitted to slavery, and how this led to tribes adopting certain customs to protect themselves. When a young girl was caught by slavers, and she had a baby with her, they would often show the baby no mercy, throwing it away in the bush for the wild animals to devour. In order to protect the children, the custom evolved that the father removed the baby to the safety of his tribal kraal. Except for the period of breastfeeding, biological mothers rarely experienced the pleasure of rearing their own children.

'The slave trade was the scourge of Africa for centuries. In some cases,' Bettie's father tells her, 'mutilation of the body was another defence against slavery.' The slave traders wanted people with strong, healthy and attractive bodies and faces. Disfigured and scarred bodies and faces repulsed the traders. Some tribes distended their lips with huge ivory or metal discs or weighed down their legs with cumbersome bangles to make themselves unattractive.

Tokyo, 1969

On her seventeenth birthday, Yoriko is officially informed by her sumi-e teacher that she is regarded as fully qualified in this art form. She can now work as an assistant to a registered artist.

It is the year before the World Expo, which is scheduled to take place in Osaka, and there is worldwide interest in all things Japanese.

Her teacher is totally taken by the talent and dedication of his student and wishes her great success in future. He sends her government qualification diploma by special messenger to a friend, also an artist, who lives in the centre of the tourist route.

The friend replies swiftly. He writes that he considers himself to be entirely unworthy of the honour bestowed on him by the illustrious teacher. However, should the gifted student feel inclined to make herself available, he would be grateful if she would attend to the tourists who gather around the stall in the street where his paintings are on sale.

Yoriko is delighted when her teacher tells her she has been accepted by the artist as an assistant. Each morning she dresses with great care in the special kimono her mother has hand-sewn for her in readiness for the World Expo celebrations the following year.

Her work consists of unpacking the paintings and displaying them to their best advantage. Dressed in her kimono, she attracts tourists, who flock to the stall.

Her gentle manner and obvious delight at being able to offer them these original works of art impress the tourists and many take out their wallets to buy something they did not plan on buying. Later in the day, she reports back to the studio of her teacher, where she spends some time making copies of the work of the great masters. If he considers them worthy, the teacher accepts them and puts his official government stamp on them, signifying his approval that they may be sold as genuine, hand-painted works of art.

One afternoon when she arrives at her teacher's home, he greets her with his customary solemn dignity. She bows deeply from the waist and remains in this position for much longer than it takes a Westerner to shake hands.

When he says her name, she hears the lilting note on which he pronounces the last syllable. This portends good news. But, true to her training, Yoriko keeps her head bowed while he speaks.

'A wealthy merchant to whom you sold one of the paintings of my much respected friend was impressed by your courteous manner. He asked the artist about your qualifications, and was referred to me. He sent a messenger with a special invitation asking me to meet him in his museum.

'We had a lengthy conversation about your eligibility, and he told me that he has a vacancy in his centre. He has graciously decided to offer you this position. You will sell the works of art on display in the museum section. He is extremely generous, and he will allow you to display some of your own paintings alongside the items in his collection. In this way, you may be lucky enough to earn some extra money. For this privilege, he will charge you only a very small percentage of the selling price of your own work.'

As her teacher speaks, a fire roars to life in Yoriko's mind. Oyo be praised! Her many prayers have been answered. She is to be acknowledged as a professional artist – a great honour for a woman.

The cultural centre is magnificent. Elegant statuettes and carvings of semi-precious stones are displayed in glass cases along the centre of the hall, and priceless tapestries and silk paintings adorn the walls. There are exquisite jade figurines in many subtle colours to delight and satisfy the most avid collector.

There are delicately translucent figurines carved from rose quartz and boxes with mosaic inlays in woods of differing hues and textures, lacquered to perfection. The silk embroideries are so finely stitched that they resemble watercolour paintings.

All these are on display for those who appreciate meticulous craftsmanship. Yoriko is intrigued by her surroundings and truly thankful that she can look after these valuable treasures. Selling her own work next to this glorious elegance gives her the inspiration every artist needs and craves.

She smiles at the tourists, sharing their pleasure at being able to handle these priceless objects. Except for a few words and phrases in English, she does not understand any of the foreign languages, but she makes an attempt at conversation by bowing respectfully and greeting them.

Yoriko is soon looking for something more to advance her education. As a student who has immersed herself in sumi-e painting, she knows that her general education lags behind. She asks permission to read some of the books from the library section of the cultural centre. She reads about foreign countries and people, and the more she reads the more sympathetic she becomes towards the many different tourists trying to make sense of a culture that is so different from their own.

She trains herself to listen carefully when people speak to her, and with her intuitive abilities often gains insight into the meaning of the foreign words uttered by the tourists. As time passes, an increasing number of her own paintings are sold. This success boosts her self-confidence.

Tsjisji, the woman who worked for her family when she

was younger, comes to the centre quite often. Sometimes she brings along some of her charges – girls who have been studying to become geishas since a young age. Yoriko loves these visits, which give her the opportunity to laugh and converse with girls her own age.

From them she hears about the idiosyncrasies of the men that come to visit them. The girls are ever hopeful that they will become the special companion of some rich man who will hire them to help him enjoy his evenings away from home. They discuss training in social graces and the beautiful clothes they have to wear. They also speak extensively about breasts. Everyone knows that it is essential for a geisha to have small breasts. Only vulgar women have large breasts.

A successful geisha has to be aware of a man's every needs. She has to be gracious in her manner of serving him during a leisurely meal and so well-versed in relating entertaining anecdotes that his mind is completely distracted from the worries of his everyday world.

A geisha makes no demands, nor does she have personal desires. Her sensuality is but a means of expressing her willingness to satisfy a man's every whim and desire. For these sexual privileges, he arranges that she comes to his house at a convenient time, or he sets her up in a little flat where she must remain faithful to him. The sole purpose of the geisha's life is to please her lover for as long as she finds favour with him. As no man will marry below his class, these girls take great pains to be extremely accomplished. They are well-read and can speak with assurance on a number of topics.

The modern young women who do not want to get married before they complete their studies are regarded as being doomed to subservience in their places of work. These women become fiercely loyal towards the people who employ them. They do not consider the life of the geisha appropriate for them, but they often need extra money – Japanese women are not rewarded as are males in the workplace. When they become desperate for cash, society does not frown upon a girl who spends a night in one of the houses frequented by impotent old men. Here a female student or a woman who considers herself to be liberated can sell her body for the night with the assurance that she will not be molested in any way.

On arrival at the house, she is given a potion to make her sleep. When she is fast asleep, an impotent man will pay handsomely for the pleasure of undressing her with the help of an assistant.

Once undressed, the old man will take a seat by the bed, looking at the sleeping young woman. When the man remembers his virile days, tears will run down his cheeks as he mourns his lost youth.

At the cultural centre, many wealthy men have fallen under the spell of Yoriko's work and some return many times to buy her paintings. But Yoriko fantasises about a master painter who will ask her to help him with his work.

She has become enchanted with the works she has seen of Ni Tsan, the famous fourteenth-century Chinese artist who is regarded as one of the four great masters of the Yuan dynasty. He gave up his worldly possessions to become a Taoist monk and a wanderer, travelling on land, sea and river. He drew what he saw and in Yoriko his works evoke a longing for a glimpse of faraway places.

In the meantime, Yoriko spends her days in the cultural centre. Whenever she needs a new kimono, she writes to her mother describing exactly the colour the embossed silk should be and giving her detailed instructions on what she would like to have embroidered on the obi, the wide sash that is tied in a complicated way around the body. Her mother calculates the cost of the material, making sure that she impresses on Yoriko how much pleasure she derives from being able to hand-sew these garments for her daughter while her eyesight is still perfect. Yoriko earns the money for her new kimonos by secretly spending some nights in a brothel for impotent old men.

Potchefstroom, 1937

Andries Venter, the farmer who has been so good to the people in the road camp, is slowly trying to pick up the pieces after the devastating drought and the economic depression of the early 1930s.

Two years before he built a school room on his farm and hired a Christian teacher to tutor his three sons privately. In this way he saved on the costs of sending his children away to boarding school, and they could help him on the farm.

But when the rains come, Venter decides to send his two older boys to boarding school. Only the youngest, Jan, remains on the farm. The boy has one year of primary school education left.

Andries speaks to Bossie and suggests that Kleinbaas, who turned four in December, attend school with Jan. It will make the task of the teacher more interesting if he has to teach a child at kindergarten level.

Kleinbaas is big for his age. He is also highly intelligent and speaks Sotho fluently. However, Bossie has noticed that his son is less fluent in Afrikaans, his mother tongue. Realising that this is a great opportunity for his son to be exposed to formal education in his own language, Bossie accepts Venter's offer.

In the mornings Anna and Boy walk with him to school.

Anna carries his satchel while the two boys run across the veld with their dogs.

When they arrive at the school room, Kleinbaas's dog Zulu takes up his position at the door where he waits patiently for his young master, whilst Boy's dog Blackie trots back home with Anna and Boy. The two return at noon to fetch Kleinbaas. If the sun is hot, or if Kleinbaas seems too tired to walk, Anna lifts him onto her back and carries him to camp.

As time passes and Kleinbaas becomes more proficient in Afrikaans, he starts to copy the mannerisms of Jan Venter. But Jan never becomes a playmate in the same way as Boy.

Kleinbaas and Boy remain inseparable and during the long summer months they spend a lot of time playing on the riverbank and in the water.

The water games invariably end with Kleinbaas pouncing on Boy, ducking him under the water, and taking him prisoner. He especially enjoys tying Boy to a small tree and dancing around him while he utters war cries.

To Kleinbaas's delight, the dogs sometimes attack each other when they hear the shouts. While Boy desperately tries to separate them, Kleinbaas eggs them on, laughing. The dogs often sustain serious wounds. Bettie Bosch does not approve of this cruelty. Her heart goes out to the dog when Zulu limps back to camp time and again after a fight with Blackie.

When Bettie complains to her husband, Bossie reacts by taking a sjambok and giving both boys a few lashes. But Boy gets one or two lashes extra. 'Because,' Bossie says, 'Boy is older and supposed to look after Kleinbaas.'

Kleinbaas cannot imagine life without Boy. Nonetheless, he feels superior to his friend simply because he is white and he has grown up with people who believe that black people are not equal to them

Every evening, before tucking him in for the night, Bettie first listens to her son's prayers. One evening he suddenly opens his eyes mid-prayer.

'Ma, will Boy also go to heaven when he dies?'

When Bettie replies that Boy will not go to heaven, because only white people go to heaven, Kleinbaas is quiet for a few seconds before continuing.

'Boy says he will stay with me forever, and work for me, and clean my shoes. What will I do if I die, and he cannot come and clean my shoes in heaven?'

Bettie laughs and replies that he should not worry about this as he will not be wearing shoes in heaven. Angels do not wear shoes.

Kleinbaas benefits greatly from the classes he attends at the farm school, and even though he is just beginning to learn to write on a slate, he surprises his mother when he shows her the lifelike drawings he makes of animals.

Sometimes some of the Sotho children from the native village a few miles away come to fetch him and Boy to play football with them. The boys will run for the ball, bump into each other and cling together, their arms slipping over their sweaty bodies while they try to manoeuvre the ball away from each other, scrabbling wildly with their feet and kicking up dust clouds. After such a wild game, they all go down to the river for a swim, stripping off their clothes and jumping naked into the water. But sometimes Kleinbaas prefers going back home. His father has rigged up a shower under one of the trees. When Kleinbaas wants to shower, he tells Boy to ask his mother for boiling water. He then undresses quickly, and, while Boy pours hot water over him, he soaps his body.

Potchefstroom, 1939

The carefree days in the road camp is soon to end as World War II breaks out in Europe in 1939. Although the fighting is far away from South Africa, it is the topic at every dinner party and around every campfire. The war is also discussed at the road camp. At night, Kleinbaas can hear his mother and father talking from his stretcher under the trees.

His parents have started to argue frequently. Their arguments become even fiercer after the visit from Oom Piet, his mother's brother, who works on the goldmines in Johannesburg. Oom Piet urges Bossie to take the red oath to show allegiance to Britain. He is concerned that Bossie is German.

'If you do not show allegiance to the British and join the army, they will soon come to fetch you and put you in a concentration camp,' he says.

His father answers that if nobody joined the army, the people of the country could unite and in this way ensure that South Africa remained neutral.

'The people who fight for the British are those who come from England and still call that country their home,' says his mother. 'The war is overseas. It has nothing to do with us. The British just want us to go and fight their war for them. We will die in our thousands. It is madness to allow such a great loss of our fellow Afrikaners.'

Kleinbaas has never heard his mother talk so much and in such a loud voice. She shouts at his father, 'You are South African, and I don't want you to fight anybody unless the war comes onto South African soil. Then you can fight.'

Men in uniform do eventually come and take his father away. His mother packs him some food and seems calm. But after Bossie leaves, she breaks down and cries. She conjures up pictures of her husband wasting away in a concentration camp. She firmly believes that he will end up just like his grandfather who was emotionally and physically damaged when he came back from the concentration camp after the Anglo Boer War.

Bettie feels the need for her parents' support. She packs up her family's belongings and she and her son move to town for a while. Anna and Boy are left behind in the camp.

Potchefstroom, 1940

Kleinbaas's whole life is turned upside down.

He feels uncomfortable when his grandfather starts to point out the faults of the Germans. It makes him feel uneasy that his father is not there to speak up for himself. He does not understand why everybody says his father is a German. He knows that everybody hates the Germans, but his father is not really a German. Yes, his father's family is German, but he rarely speaks German.

Trying to make sense of what is happening Kleinbaas often walks along the bank of the Mooi River flowing through Potchefstroom. He soon becomes friendly with some black youths to whom he speaks in perfect Sotho. He is comfortable in their presence and always feels much happier after spending time with them.

Sometimes some of the young black girls join them and the boys chase them and roll in the grass with them. The girls always put up a half-hearted fight. But everybody knows it is fun and that the boys like the game as much as the girls. When Kleinbaas catches a girl, he flings her to the ground and orders her to lie still before lying on top of her.

During their stay in Potchefstroom his mother tells him that he should not fight with his girl cousins, who come to live with Oupa and Ouma after their father goes to war.

Bettie tells Kleinbaas that it is a sin to think of any girl in such a way that it makes you feel strange 'down there'. However, Kleinbaas is constantly thinking of girls without their clothes on and it seems as if he always has a strange feeling down there.

His mother's words scare him so much that he can scarcely look at his cousins. He feels incredibly shy in their presence.

However, he is not shy when he is amongst the black girls. But he can tell nobody of the games he and the Sotho boys play with them. He often hears his grandfather say that it would be a terrible disgrace to have to admit that you slept with a black girl.

Kleinbaas also knows that although his mother loves Anna

and Boy, she has never thought of them as being her equals. They have their own cups and plates back at the veld camp and Anna is not allowed to wash her clothes with those of the Bosch family.

After a few months Bossie is released quite unexpectedly.

Bossie writes to the government, asking if he can be reinstated in his old job. The response is positive, but he is informed that he is to be transferred to a camp close to Potgietersrus in the Northern Transvaal.

This suits Bettie and she agrees to follow her husband to yet another camp. But Bettie is worried that Kleinbaas will miss Boy's company.

Before they leave for Potgietersrus, Bossie and his family go to their old camp to say goodbye to the Venters and Bossie's team. Bettie asks Anna to move with them, but Anna declines. She has decided to go to Johannesburg to look for Boy's father. Bettie has no choice but to accept Anna's decision.

The two women say a teary farewell. Anna has become much more than a servant to Bettie. She has been a companion in the lonely camp.

Potgietersrus, 1948

The new camp in Potgietersrus is set in beautiful surroundings with huge boekenhout, milkwoods and wild fig trees along the banks of the river.

Kleinbaas loves the landscape and the open air lifestyle. This bushveld camp is the place he would later refer to as home. There are two other tents. The first is used by the foreman Boet Schoombie and his wife, Alie, and their children. In the second tent live two young white road workers, while the third tent is shared by Bossie and Bettie. Kleinbaas chooses a cosy clump of bushes under which he puts his stretcher and the paraffin box he uses as a table.

Bettie's fears about Kleinbaas being isolated are allayed when she sees how readily he makes friends with the Schoombie boys. She is proud and relieved to hear from Alie Schoombie that her children are impressed by the authoritative manner in which Kleinbaas approaches the native children that they visit in the nearby kraals.

He grows into a healthy and attractive sixteen-year-old. He loves the sounds of the veld at night. The monotonous call of a night bird drifts him off to sleep after a busy day of hunting and playing in the veld. He is used to the grunts and growls of the nocturnal hunters sneaking through the grass foraging for food. Sometimes the roar of a lion, the hysterical laughter of a hyena and the grunting of a wildebeest merge like a symphony of concerted sounds. He has no fear of the night noises. Alone on his stretcher he feels completely at ease – he feels part of the African landscape.

In this new camp, Bossie is still in charge of the work gang, while Bettie and Alie cook for the men. During the week Kleinbaas and the three Schoombie children stay at the hostel in Potgietersrus where they attend school. They are brought back to the camp each Friday by the railway bus. As soon as they get home, the children disappear into the veld where they hunt for rabbits with a few of the local children from the nearby village. Having grown up in the veld with Boy, Kleinbaas is an expert at hunting. The Schoombie boys look up to him and envy his fluency in Sotho. Even though he is the youngest of the three, he is always chosen as the leader when they are invited by the local children to play ball games with them.

They make catapults and bows and arrows which they use to shoot birds and small animals. They fight battles in which the white children represent the Afrikaners and the black children the Communists or Nazis.

At school the children speak Afrikaans, but they are divided into groups along church and political allegiance lines. The different groups shout derogatory remarks at each other, and when things get heated, two group leaders will square up to each other in a fistfight.

Over the weekends, the men get involved in heated arguments around the campfire. Living an uneventful rural life, the men talk mostly about the political situation in South Africa. As Afrikaners, they are proud of the fact that the National Party has seized control of the country, thus breaking the hold of the British over South Africa. Some of the men believe it is a good thing that the National Party has passed strict laws enforcing the segregation of black and white people.

They argue over the way this policy of apartheid is being criticised all over the world. Kleinbaas listens to the men saying that it is all right for the English to criticise because they still have their British passports and can easily go back to England. But the Afrikaners have nowhere else to go. They speak a language that has developed on African soil, and they have become Africans even though they are white.

Holidays are still divided between the Fouriesburg where Oupa Bosch lives and Potchefstroom where Oupa Kruger lives. Both grandfathers have strong opinions about the Afrikaners, and they love sharing their thoughts. Kleinbaas has acquired his mother's habit of listening to them without commenting. When he becomes bored, he simply tunes out their voices while pretending to listen. Oupa Kruger sits in his chair on the step of the boarding house in Potchefstroom and says, 'The trouble with the Afrikaners is that we are too easily attracted by the shining things of this world. Now that we are in power, we want to be just like the English. Our black pots and pans are no good anymore, now we must have imported ones from England.'

And Oupa Bosch will invite Kleinbaas to take walks with him into the veld. While they sit on a rock overlooking the magnificent mountain ranges and deep green valleys, Oupa Bosch will put a hand on Kleinbaas's knee and say, 'Ja, my son, life is not easy. But the trouble with the Afrikaner is that they want things to come easy. They don't want to work. They think they can walk into the veld and shoot a buck and look at their ostriches and get rich, and they think that is work! They don't know that it takes hard work and an empty stomach before you get your money. Like the ostriches, you have to eat stones to get good feathers.' And he screws up his eyes, and his shoulders shake with laughter.

Kleinbaas notices that his father has become quieter. It is as if he is ashamed of expressing an opinion in public. He seems happy only when he is with the road workers. And it seems his slight German accent is getting more pronounced with age.

At home his mother does most of the talking now, in a quiet, consoling sort of way, while his father answers in a flat, resigned and dispassionate manner.

Kleinbaas is an average scholar, with no particular interest in any subject at school. However, he is popular because of his talent at drawing. The other children are fascinated by his ability to make quick caricature sketches of the teacher or other pupils, satirically emphasising their faults.

He also makes drawings of the genitals of the black girls that he meets in secret during the weekends when he is at the camp.

He is getting more restless every weekend. His mother's nagging reminder on Sundays that he has to go to church, when he would rather go into the veld, is getting on his nerves.

He sees a possible way out when one of his mother's brothers promises him that he will get him a job on the mines if he passes his Junior Certificate examination. The uncle also offers him accommodation at his house in Mayfair, Johannesburg.

But Basie is not sure that he wants to take up this offer. He remembers his Oupa Bosch saying to him, 'Ja, son, if you want to make money, you must go where the money is, and that is where the English are. They've put their money into this country, and no matter what the Afrikaners think, the country now belongs to them. The English will keep their big business money in their own hands. They'll never let the Afrikaners take over the administration of the goldmines or the diamond mines.'

~

Johannesburg, 1950

When he arrives in Johannesburg, his uncle wastes no time in taking him to his place of work – one of the goldmines surrounding the city. But as the lift cage opens up to take the men down the shaft, Kleinbaas gets a whiff of the stale damp air. His throat constricts and he cannot breathe. He rushes into the open air and refuses to go back. He cannot imagine going into the bowels of the earth and working there all day long.

Soon after his experience at the mine, he wanders onto a building site in Mayfair quite by accident. Living in the veld all those years, Kleinbaas had often observed his father making furniture or fixing things around the camp, and had thus picked up his father's carpentry skills.

He asks around at the site in Mayfair and is directed to the contractor, John Miller. Kleinbaas introduces himself as Bill, the shortened, English version of his second name, Willem. Miller hires him as an apprentice carpenter, but when, a few weeks after he starts working, Miller hears Bill speaking fluently in Sotho to some of the workers, he immediately puts him in charge of the black labourers. Whenever he needs to travel to an area where he knows the people cannot speak English, he takes Bill along as an interpreter.

Bill is happy working for Miller. The burly man from London has a thick Cockney accent. Bill finds it far more interesting than the Afrikaans accents of his relatives.

Bill quickly adapts to the pace of city life. On Saturdays and Sundays he visits the pool hall in Fordsburg where he meets men from all walks of life. With his mother's blue eyes and his father's dark hair and complexion, he is an attractive young man who draws appreciative glances from women.

Sometimes his uncle visits him and urges him to go to church and spend the Sunday with their family, but he prefers his independence, and usually makes an excuse.

The rooms of the boarding house where he stays in Mayfair open out onto a back stoep and it does not take him long to notice that the servant girls working in the house share a room across the yard at the back of the building. He sets his sights on one young woman. She laughs when he uses the explicit sexual phrases he's learnt from the Sotho boys back home.

A few days after he speaks to her for the first time, she agrees to have sex with him for a certain amount of money. It is the height of the apartheid regime, and it is illegal for men and women of different races to have sexual intercourse. Even so, Bill has no qualms about letting the woman into his bedroom.

He demands sex frequently, and he threatens her with dismissal should she ever report him to the police. He soon becomes bored with the woman, but she is the only female he has recourse to for instant satisfaction.

He still fears approaching Afrikaans girls and he is initially too shy to talk to the English girls, although the few he meets always seem to find him entertaining.

Remembering what his Oupa Bosch had told him, he decides that he will marry an English girl one day. He even takes to reading *The Outspan*, an English magazine, to find out what the English girls are interested in.

When he mentions the magazine and his plans to marry an English girl to his mother, she is immediately concerned about him wasting money on reading material. Especially English books. She advises him to read the Bible and tells him that not all English people are Christian. Only the Protestants are. Those who are of the Catholic faith are, according to Bettie, not Christian.

'They do not worship God the way us Afrikaners do,' she says. After a moment of contemplation she adds: 'But if you really intend to go on reading, you should join a library, because the books in the library are all good books that have been passed by the censor, and you don't have to waste money on buying them.'

While browsing in a second-hand bookshop in Fordsburg, he finds a book on Eastern sexuality which immediately fires his imagination. He is mesmerised by the erotic pictures and the descriptions of the different ways a woman can please a man 'the Oriental way'. He tries to get the servant girl to do the things that he has read about, but she only giggles and demands more money.

To hide his feeling of foolishness, he pins her down on the bed and hits her in the face with his open hand. He is instantly aroused by his own violence and the feeling of power he has over the woman lying beneath him.

At work, his boss sees some of the architectural sketches Bill has made of the buildings on which they work. The contractor promotes him to the drawing office where he is immediately at home as a draughtsman.

With the increase in his salary, Bill can afford to move from the lodging house to a small flat in Doornfontein. He also becomes more discerning about his clothes, adopting a style that marks him as a progressive man about town. He walks with a determined swagger and when he smiles his cheeks are pushed into perpendicular lines on the sides of his mouth. His smile and self-confidence make him irresistible to women.

∽

Johannesburg, 1954

The National Party's policy of apartheid is in full swing. Bill cannot believe his luck when he lands a job at a construction company with a government contract for building segregated sub-economic township houses for black people. One day, early in the year, his boss John Miller asks him to bring some of his terrain worksheets to his home in Parktown, a wealthy part of Johannesburg.

When Bill arrives at the palatial house, his boss introduces him to a girl who is visiting. She is slightly built and reminds him of a feathery brown owl – something soft that would shrivel up the moment it felt threatened. He speaks kindly to her, aware of a sense of protectiveness that he has not previously felt for another person.

He is genuinely sorry to hear that both her parents, who were friends of the boss's, had died in a car accident. He listens keenly when she tells him she was the only beneficiary of their estate, which included a big house in Parktown. He immediately offers to help if she needs work done around the house. He tells her he could arrange for members of his work gang to go to the house.

When he does not hear from her within the first week after meeting her, he takes the trouble to find out where she lives and drops by one Saturday afternoon, making quite sure that he takes two of the black labourers and a lawn mower with him. He soon convinces her that it would be a pleasure for his 'boys' to mow the lawn and clean the swimming pool while he sits with her on the veranda drinking tea.

In no time, he becomes a regular visitor to Parktown. And instead of going to the pool hall on Saturday afternoons, he spends the day drinking tea. After a few months Bill moves into the house as a lodger. He convinces Mable that it would be easier for him to supervise the work around the house and garden if he lived on the premises.

Within a short time he has ingratiated himself with her so completely that a marriage proposal is inevitable. When he proposes, Mable accepts immediately. That she is ten years older than him does not bother him at all, and she seems to thrive on the fact that she has managed to catch such a good-looking young man.

Soon after they have exchanged wedding vows, Bill makes

it clear that he does not intend to spend every weekend of his life drinking tea with her. He starts frequenting the pool hall again.

Before his wedding he goes to Potchefstroom to tell his maternal grandfather about his upcoming marriage. He believes that his grandfather would not approve of him getting married to an Englishwoman, but he is surprised when the old man speaks up in her favour.

'Anglicans are very devout people,' says his grandfather. 'And it is a good thing that you have chosen somebody who can persuade you to go to church on Sundays. It really does not matter which church you go to – the woman is the boss of the house, and I am happy that you will have a Christian wife that you can respect.'

In the early days of his marriage to Mable, Bill undresses with typical youthful unconcern, letting his clothes lie on the floor where they fall. As a non-confrontational way of teaching him some manners, Mable kicks the clothes under the bed. A week later, when he finds his cupboard empty, he turns to her, asking, 'What happened to my clothes?' She replies, 'I don't know. Where did you last leave them?' He opens cupboards and drawers, until she eventually suggests, 'Why don't you look under the bed?'

When he realises what Mable has done, he turns on her

in cold fury, shouting that he would be better off living with 'one of the blacks'. He orders her to see that the servants do their work properly, sweeping under the beds and picking up after him, otherwise she would soon find herself alone at night.

Mable is extremely surprised at this show of anger from him, but reason tells her that she is older and better educated, and this might have made him feel at a disadvantage and caused his frustration to turn to anger. She adopts a long-suffering yet considerate manner towards him, but as time passes this also infuriates him and adversely affects their sexual relationship, a factor of prime importance in his life.

Within a few months after his marriage he starts to join a group of fellow workmen on trips over the border to Basutoland, where they indulge in wild drinking parties with 'black diamonds', as they euphemistically call the Sotho prostitutes. Afterwards he returns home with a swagger and a feeling of superiority.

Johannesburg, 1960

Driving along in Fordsburg one day, Bill sees a young, luscious blonde with a tip-tilted nose and a cheeky smile standing on the side of the road. On the spur of the moment he pulls up, leans over, opens the car door, and calling to her in Afrikaans, offers to give her a lift to wherever she wants to go. The girl accepts and, getting into the car, introduces herself as Dolly.

She tells him she is sixteen years old, an orphan who has run away from her foster family. He wants to know if the police are looking for her, but she assures him that her foster parents would be only too pleased to see the back of her.

He takes her to Doornfontein, where he knows a woman who sometimes obliges him by allowing him the use of a room for an afternoon. He books Dolly in for the night.

It is clear that Bill is not her first lover. For hours on end she matches his lust until eventually she complains that she is hungry. He arranges for her to stay in the house for the weekend. During their sexual romps, he teaches her all the tricks he has read about in his sex manual. She seems to enjoy every minute and by the end of the weekend, she is clearly in love with him.

Bill decides not to lose this young girl who enjoys sex as much as he does, and so he rents her a small bachelor flat near his office.

In search of greater excitement, Bill one day suggests to Dolly that she gets a black girl to join their Saturday afternoon sexual games. But she refuses, bursting into tears and saying that she does not want to get caught and go to jail.

Demanding the real reason for her refusal, Bill eventually gets Dolly to admit that she has been chased away by her birth parents because of a miscarriage. They accepted the fact that their fourteen-year-old daughter had fallen pregnant out of wedlock, but to their horror, the foetus had been black.

In a rage, her father assaulted her, and demanded the name of the father so that he could shoot the bastard. Her father then threatened to phone the police and have her put in jail.

She ran away to Johannesburg and had just arrived in the city when Bill picked her up. She will love him for the rest of her life, she tells him, but pleads that he not ask her to do anything that involves sex with black people, as this could land her in jail.

After a few months of maintaining Dolly, Bill urges her to get out of the flat and start earning some money. He wants her to become less dependent on him. He might get bored of her, and then she'd become a problem. He encourages her to speak English and gets her a job working for a Greek in a café near the flat.

Johannesburg, 1961

South Africa becomes a republic. While the celebrations are in full swing, Dolly discovers that she is three months pregnant. She demands that Bill buys her a wedding ring. She knows about Mable and that Bill would never leave his wife. But she does not want to have to answer uncomfortable questions about her ringless finger and her huge belly.

'Tell whoever asks that you are married to a Mister Brown,' Bill says as he slips the cheap ring onto her finger. 'Tell them that your husband is working abroad.'

When the child is born, they name her Ellen. Bill accepts the child as his own, but notices that a change has come over Dolly. She has becomes more assertive and argumentative, and she starts to put on weight.

She now demands that he pay for a bigger flat – the bachelor flat has become too small to accommodate a baby as well. Bill has to hire a black woman to look after Ellen during the day while Dolly is working. This arrangement suits them both as Dolly has no idea how to rear a child, and prefers to work. Bill often visits the baby during the day and very soon secures himself the added benefit of free sex with the nanny, warning her to keep her mouth shut.

Tokyo, 1972

A foreigner approaches Yoriko. When he is close, she feels a jolt of recognition. She knows she has never in her life seen this attractive stranger, but she immediately knows that he will become important to her. She looks shyly at him as he speaks to her.

He is clearly several years older than her, but Yoriko feels strangely elated. His proud bearing and confidence overwhelm her. For a few moments she is unable to utter even one of the few English words and phrases she has painstakingly memorised. On a sudden impulse she picks up a brush lying on the worktable and dips it in ink.

Today she will not wave to the department's interpreter to translate the words of this handsome stranger to her. She quickly makes a few ink sketches on a sheet of rice paper. There is a little house around which she draws a circle clearly symbolising earth. At the northernmost tip she adds the North Star before drawing the Southern.

She draws a question mark next to the house before looking up. Lifting her eyebrows she asks: 'You home?'

With an engaging smile and a debonair sweep of his arm, Bill takes the brush from her hand and, after dipping it in ink, draws a map of Africa. He makes a cross at the southern end of the continent and, holding a hand over his heart, bows to her, smiling. With girlish laughter she in turn places the palms of her hands together and makes a deep, welcoming bow. She holds out her left hand and with the other points to her engagement finger. The question is obvious. Is he in any way involved with somebody? But is she asking if he is engaged or married, or simply whether he has a woman?

He feels desire rising. Last night's visit to a massage parlour has whetted his appetite and brought home to him that every hour, every moment on this short package tour of the Orient, is precious and not to be wasted. He feasts his eyes on the delicate beauty of this Japanese girl.

He is determined not to let her slip through his fingers. This little doll is so different from his mistress or his wife. His mistress, Dolly, seems incredibly coarse in comparison to her and he has never made it a secret that he married Mable, a frail Englishwoman, only for her money.

Bill finishes his drawings and looks up at Yoriko dressed in her exquisite kimono. She looks as fragile as a piece of translucent bone china.

Yoriko is enthralled. This beautiful man handles her paintbrush like an expert. Covering the rice paper with free brush strokes, he draws trees and landscapes and animals quite different from those that she has seen in Japan.

Taking a new sheet of paper, Bill once again dips the brush

in ink. With her heart fluttering, Yoriko recognises a house and a woman lying in bed and a little girl sitting next to the woman crying. He also draws a coffin and a grave and a big question mark.

Yoriko's eyes mirror her sorrow. Is this his wife? Is she ill and dying, or perhaps dead already? A great artist needs an understanding wife, for surely this man is a great artist in his own country?

They communicate for some time in this manner. She offers him tea and Bill smiles and pats her arm. She allows him this contact, although such familiarity is not usually tolerated by Japanese women. At the end of their conversation, he holds a hand out to her and asks her if she could accompany him while he explores the city.

Yoriko can think of nothing she would rather do, but she shakes her head and gestures to the art displayed around them. In the few words of English she knows, she tries to explain that she has to work.

He looks around and sees a male assistant, whom he beckons to come closer. The man bows, thinking Yoriko has made a sale, and enquires in a singsong voice which piece he is interested in. Bill explains that he wants Yoriko to show him the sights of the city. The man smiles, bowing his head, while explaining that she is a shop assistant and there are other girls who would be delighted to show him around. Bill is adamant. He does not want another girl showing him the sights. It has to be this one. The man turns to Yoriko and they enter into a rapid-fire exchange which stops as suddenly as it had started.

Smiling at Bill the man says that Yoriko knows nothing about the city, but would be delighted to show him the gardens and temples next Sunday on her day off.

'Next Sunday!' he explodes indignantly. He has only four days to spend in this city. By next Sunday he will be gone. He holds up four fingers while staring intently at the man. The man, still nodding his head and smiling, says he is very sorry but it is impossible.

'Impossible?' Bill replies. 'Nothing is impossible!'

He asks for the manager who eventually arrives smiling and bowing. Yoriko notices that Bill is forceful in his arguments, speaking to the manager with imperative gestures. She admires those samurai qualities in him and is pleased to see that the manager nods his head in agreement. Turning to her, the manager mutters under his breath in Japanese: 'These foreigners have money.'

Speaking clearly again he says to Bill: 'The tourist is important and welcome in Japan.' He would gladly give Yoriko one week's leave without pay, starting immediately, he says.

He again turns to Yoriko and in his mother tongue tells

her that she is very lucky to be given all this time off. He emphasises that he expects her to bring the foreigner back to the shop so that he may buy the gifts that he says he wants to take back to South Africa. Yoriko bows her head and thanks the manager graciously in Japanese.

During her studies as a sumi-e artist, Yoriko has assimilated the teachings of Zen. She has spent hours meditating in order to achieve a state of utter calm. But now, with Bill standing close to her, there is little left of her serenity. Where is her clear inner vision? Why is her heart pounding in her ears?

The interpreter tells Bill that he has to accompany them, both for propriety's sake and to translate when Yoriko cannot find the words.

'Tonight we will dine in a fashionable restaurant where the geisha hostess will take good care of everybody,' he says in English before translating the words for Yoriko.

'Yes, yes,' she nods eagerly.

Later, in the restaurant, Bill compliments Yoriko on her beautiful eyes and with great self-assurance he orders more food, more wine, more music. She lifts her lashes shyly, stealing a sidelong glance at him. He is rich, he is handsome, he is in the prime of his life and gives orders as one born into the noble class.

When he tells her that he is a famous painter known by

everybody in his own country, Yoriko is delighted. Truly she is the lucky one. The Clever One is favoured by the ancestors.

Bill is fully aware of the effect he is having on her. He looks at her blatantly, his eyes lingering on her breasts with a teasing, suggestive smile. He feels a rush of excitement when he sees the blush spreading over her face as she lowers her eyes. He grins triumphantly at the interpreter, relishing the power he has over women.

He has heard that the Japanese do not invite strangers into their homes. But he wants to see the inside of the house where Yoriko lives. If he can gain entry to the house, it will be something to boast about back home.

He turns to the guide: 'Tell her I want to take photographs of her and her home to cheer up a girl who is sad because her mother is very ill.'

Bill sees Yoriko's eyes fill with sorrow as the guide speaks to her. She places her hands together and bows deeply. It is clear that she believes his story and promises to arrange it for him.

Bill cannot hide his excitement. He reminds Yoriko of a little boy and it makes her smile.

After a while he explains to the guide that he wants to see some of the other sights on offer in their city. He suggests a visit to a nightclub.

Yoriko does not find the request strange. It is customary

for men in her country to go out alone at night. If he wants to spend time with some of the geishas it will be her pleasure to see that his wishes are granted. She flutters around Bill, putting up her hand to her face to hide the gleam of her perfect white teeth, in case he should find her smile immodest.

When the taxi stops in front of the nightclub she hurries forward and stands with bowed head at the entrance while Bill and the interpreter enter, then follows immediately behind them. The manager leads them to a private entertainment room where they are joined by two geisha girls. Yoriko is still dressed in her traditional kimono which she has to wear for her work at the cultural centre. She compares favourably with the exquisite geisha girls whose faces are powdered and painted to perfection in their elaborate kimonos.

Yoriko talks to them animatedly, telling them that the manager has requested a 'special' for this client. Two geishas will undress him on a massage mattress and pummel his whole body, from top to toe, before taking him to a bath where he will be scrubbed rigorously.

They will then wrap him in towels, and slowly begin to unwind the towels while manipulating his erotic zones. The man is pleasured for hours, enjoying the intense sexual foreplay without the final self-destructive orgasm, in this way achieving the 'Oriental thrill' of unendurable pleasure.

Her geisha friends have at length discussed this form of pleasure with Yoriko, and she is grateful that Bill will be taken care of by experts. Rising, she takes her leave, excusing herself with many deep bows and a wish for his happiness and pleasure for the rest of the night.

The guide takes Yoriko home, where she immediately tells her aunt Kato about her unexpected happiness and her special holiday.

She tells her aunt that Bill is wonderful. He is rich. He looks like a king. He does not want to sleep with her, but wants to visit them in their home. He will buy expensive presents for them. No, he is not a doctor. Much better! He is a very famous artist. He gives commands to the managers and the guides and knows exactly what he wants.

Kato cautions her about men like Bill, but Yoriko is deaf and blind to her aunt's warnings and responds only to her emotions.

The next morning Yoriko cannot contain her excitement as she waits for Bill to arrive at her post in the cultural centre. When he eventually enters the hall, he waves at her from a distance, then talks to the manager who arranges for him to see the ancient city and many unusual sights.

Last night's pleasure was a good start, he muses. The girls

who massaged him the previous night had at first seemed too much like children, but the expert manner in which they tended to his physical desires had a certain charm that made him forget their smallness and asexual bodies.

They reminded him of his teenage daughter, Ellen, back home. He has noticed that men are starting to take notice of her. Dolly is not the ideal mother. Although Bill is not close to his daughter, he wants a better life for her than that of her mother. He doesn't want her ending up in a massage parlour or tending to other people's sexual whims like these little Japanese whores. There was a time when he could hug her tightly and believed that she was the best thing ever to tread this earth. But then she'd grown distant. Maybe she grew up too suddenly.

When he gets home he will have to give this matter of his daughter and her future some serious thought. He hates the idea that Ellen might become pregnant and end up like her mother. God knows, Ellen has not much to be proud of in her mother.

On the last day of his tour his first wish is granted. He visits Yoriko and her aunt in their home. The guide has explained that this is not at all customary, but as his stay is short and the circumstances most unusual, Yoriko insists that this personal honour be bestowed on one as famous as he. The women prepare a traditional tea ceremony and afterwards Bill sends the guide with explicit instructions to bring back many presents on approval from the cultural centre so that Yoriko and Kato have a choice. Even this request is most unusual and they laugh at the guide's discomfort. Afterwards they visit the house of Yoriko's mother, bringing her a present. Everybody is impressed by his grandeur and superior manner.

To Yoriko, the final lifting of her loosened kimono and the consummation of their passion is the ultimate realisation of her artistic and cultural imaginings. She marvels at the overwhelming power of love that he has awakened in her. While he sleeps, she carefully strokes the damp hair away from his forehead and stares at his sleeping face for a long time.

Yoriko and the guide go to the airport with him. Before Bill finally says goodbye, he promises to write frequently. He tells Yoriko that he will soon be back in her country.

The guide asks: 'Coming back to get married?' It is not the kind of question a Japanese normally asks a foreigner. But Yoriko has urged him to try to find out what Bill's future plans are.

Bill smiles and nods. 'Yes,' he says. When he returns he and Yoriko will get married. What the hell. He is on his way home, and he can make promises he does not intend to keep.

After Bill leaves, Yoriko drifts on her own private rosy cloud. She has never experienced such joy. She knows that she has encountered the love of her life and she cannot wait for them to be reunited.

Even the people in the shop look different. The faces are the same, but Yoriko has rediscovered them with a sense of warmth and awareness. The art treasures glow with an undiscovered perfection of craftsmanship, revealing some mystic depth of inner beauty. When painting, her brush touches the paper lightly, precisely as before, yet in a strangely new way.

A year drags by and she has only had one letter from Bill. Her excitement fades. Yoriko is heartbroken. At night her aunt, her sympathetic life companion, whispers to her when she cannot sleep. She urges Yoriko to work harder, to paint better, to love the people around her more sincerely. She begs Yoriko not to forget about her own people and her heritage, and not to think about the world she has glimpsed.

Tokyo, 1974

Yoriko waits for months on end for a letter from Bill. At times she is deaf and blind to her immediate surroundings and barely has enough energy to lift a paint brush.

Her hopes of hearing from the woman who visited the cultural centre and promised to find out more about Bill, fade after a few months of silence.

Her aunt Kato admonishes her. The experience with Bill is an episode that belongs to the past and is best forgotten. But Yoriko cannot let go of her memories of him.

When nearly all hope is abandoned, another letter from South Africa arrives like a shooting star. She devours it, regains her strength, and her lifeblood flows back into her heart. She has become two people: one an empty husk, a tired automaton, the other an energetic woman who suddenly comes alive when a letter arrives.

After having the letter translated, she is renewed, and spends hours and days drafting a perfect answer. But after every letter the same pattern ensues. Many months pass without a word from him, she again wilts, holding herself together during her working hours but disintegrating the moment she arrives home.

Kato also notices that Yoriko has become preoccupied with ancient rituals. When months go by without a word from the South African, she makes careful preparations to visit ancient family shrines. Miraculously, not long after these visits, a letter arrives.

Eventually her aunt finds a mountain retreat where she

takes Yoriko for a rest cure. Through her prayers she endeavours to save the girl's last vestige of pride. Yoriko also prays continuously, begging Oyo to influence the heart of her lover. When the colour returns to Yoriko's cheeks, Kato takes her back home.

However, soon after they return, Yoriko resumes visiting the shrines of her ancestors to pray. She remembers the long-ago words of the fortune-teller: 'Truth is inwardly revealed.'

Nearly three years after meeting Bill, the letter arrives that is to change her life.

She rushes to the professional letter writer who has to translate every word for her. Can she be sure that the words he translates are the same ones her lover intended for her ears only? Quickly she admonishes herself. 'Where is the faith, and the trust and the belief in the virtue and omniscience of her dear Oyo? Surely he guides the eyes and voice of this man who reads, as surely as he guides the pen of the one who writes!'

My Dearest Yoriko!

I am so sorry that your wonderful letter remained unanswered these many months. I had such a bad shock that it made me physically ill. I did not wish to trouble your pretty head with my problems. You are my life, my ray of sunshine, my only hope in this dismal darkness. I did not tell you that I had this sad burden to carry, my pretty one, for I believe that I have to bear my burdens alone. I have watched my wife become ill, and had to watch her slowly dying from this incurable disease! How I longed for the warmth of your tender breast on which to rest my weary head. I have tended to all her wishes and I have tried to help my little daughter …

Yoriko opens her eyes wide. Wife? Child? She feels her heart thumping wildly.

… Only through the strength of our love, and the hope of a future where we may be together, have I been given the will to go on living like a hermit, celibate and alone. I did not wish for her death, yet it is here hovering over our heads, like the wings of a vulture. That is the reason, my pretty one, that my letters have been few and far between.

Months of pent-up tension is released. Her shoulders shake as the tears start flowing.

'Thank you, dear Oyo, for looking after my wonderful man and keeping his love alive.'

The scribe pauses and looks at the table in front of him on which the letter lies. He rearranges the ink and the paint brushes, placing them in their correct order in the little box next to the rice paper.

Slowly Yoriko lifts her head, and he continues:

The doctors have informed me that she has unusual strength. I know you will understand that it may take months for her to die. My real concern is for my daughter, who is now thirteen years old, and at the age when she needs female love and companionship. In this country she has no relations besides this dying mother. She is a beautiful girl, as you can see from the photograph.

I have given this a lot of thought and you are the soulmate I will marry one day. So doesn't it make some sense, my dearest love, for me to send this child of mine to you, that you two get acquainted? Only for a year. The doctor says my wife won't live that long. You will one day be her mother, and at the moment she needs someone whom she can love instead of living here alone with me and this great sadness in my life.

You can instruct her in the art of flower arrangement, and prepare her for an honourable marriage. This poor child has never had the joy of experiencing the love that I know exists between you and your mother. She will be our link in love – a living promise of a future we will one day share.

I am eagerly waiting for the day we will be together again.
With all my love,
Bill Bosch

Yoriko removes the photograph from the envelope and looks at it intently. It is the picture of a beautiful young blonde girl. Yoriko recalls how she was sent to the home of her aunt after her father had died, and how her aunt has been a mother to her ever since. Surely this is what Oyo has in mind, that she may share such a love with someone young, in sincere gratitude for what she herself has received in life.

How can she refuse Bill?

Kato warns her. She points out the many cultural differences and the language barrier, which will cause many difficulties. The house is tiny and not suitable to accommodate foreign visitors. Surely Yoriko knows that her people do not easily invite strangers into their homes? The man expects the impossible. One cannot teach a foreigner the art of Ikebana in just one year.

But Yoriko listens only to the urgings of her own heart and body. She reminds her aunt that this letter and request have come as a direct answer to her prayers. Already a curse rests on this house; she should therefore not provoke the ancestors now that her wish has been granted. Should she be reluctant and refuse to help Bill, the ancestors may forsake her completely. Have not the spirits of her ancestors constantly warned them of this danger? Oyo has answered her prayer, giving light in the darkness. Her duty now is to accept the responsibility unreservedly. The years of unremitting determination to cherish her love have cemented Yoriko's wishes into an unshakable resolve to prove herself worthy of the omnipotence and care of Oyo.

Her aunt cannot find fault with such honourable arguments, and accepts the inevitable.

However, the house is too small to accommodate the child from the faraway country, and Kato has to ask the teacher who has been living with them for years to find new lodgings. Showing her respect towards him, she serves him the ceremonial dish of tea, then graciously informs him that, through the intervention of the will of their ancestor Oyo, his sojourn in their home has regrettably come to an end. The room is to be prepared for occupation by a guest from another country. The teacher listens in silence, hears that the girl is young and her mother is dying, and that she comes from that racist country, South Africa. After a while he nods his head solemnly. He understands that he has to leave and he thanks Kato for her kindness and graciousness over the years.

When the child with the unpronounceable name finally arrives, she towers above Yoriko and her aunt. She is given the name Tagenaga, The Tall One. Tagenaga's initial excitement at the opportunity to come and study in Japan soon gives way to bewilderment at the fact that the people she is to stay with cannot speak English. She finds it disconcerting that the gardens and houses are so tiny. She is clearly a stranger in an even stranger country.

One look at the young girl and Yoriko feels as if she is looking into Bill's eyes again. She starts eating normally for the first time in months. She needs to put on weight to control this young woman for whom she is prepared to sacrifice her privacy and her freedom.

She tries her best to make Tagenaga feel at home, bowing low and giving her the best of everything she has to offer. The strange language and customs terrify the young girl. How is she ever going to survive in this country? She tries to be strong, but at night when she is lying on her tatami mat, despair overwhelms her and she sobs loudly.

Out of necessity she learns the meaning of quite a large number of Japanese words. Yoriko spends hours with her trying to teach her the language, and even hires a private tutor to help her.

When Yoriko hears her crying at night, she rushes to Tagenaga's mat and cradles the homesick child in her arms, all the while stroking the golden hair and whispering words of comfort and encouragement, but never once does she refer to the impending death of the child's mother.

In the mornings she helps Tagenaga to get dressed in the complicated kimono and obi that she has to wear while she attends classes in Ikebana. Before hurrying to the cultural centre where she works, Yoriko first walks to the school with Tagenaga.

The arrival of the girl has given Yoriko a reason to smile again. Her heart is light as she paints pictures with firm strokes of the brush to the delight of the tourists who watch her work.

In the early days, Kato hurries to fetch Tagenaga from school in the afternoons and walks with her back to their home, where she supervises her schoolwork as she had supervised Yoriko's studies when she was young. After work Yoriko teaches Tagenaga how to pronounce the beautiful words of the Japanese language, helping her with the different inflections.

While learning to write, Tagenaga has to learn to recognise the many different meanings lurking in the central idea of the written ideogram.

Yoriko rediscovers the uniqueness of her own language and culture while teaching Tagenaga. She also teaches the lanky child how to sit and stand and walk like an elegant lady. In their small house there is very little space, and the girl has great difficulty in accustoming herself to the discipline of keeping her hands close to her sides and tucking her feet in under her when she sits down on the floor. She has to learn not to touch other people and always allow a small space between her and another, be it on the bus or while shopping or walking in the street or at home with Yoriko and her aunt, sitting on the floor around the central table.

Yoriko also teaches Tagenaga that a Japanese woman is always humble and can always be turned to for comfort. It is worrying to Yoriko that Ellen finds it difficult to grasp the basic truth that, of all people, men need extra care and comfort.

Men must be taken seriously under all circumstances. A woman should never make fun of them or their interests or their hobbies. The woman, though clever, must not allow herself to be drawn into arguments, but must learn to make light and cheerful conversation and remain smiling at all times.

It is her duty to relieve the man of pain and stress because of the heavy burden he carries in life. The wife must create an atmosphere in the home which allows him to forget his troubles. And should it be required that she help him in the business as well, she must remain a subordinate, demure decoration, like a sweet fragrant flower oozing elegance and feminine charm. She must allow him the pleasure and freedom to enjoy his own interests and his own life, as he wishes.

Yoriko is pleased to notice that Tagenaga is strong-willed. She reminds her of Bill. But she finds it exasperating that the young woman gets angry quickly. If she does not get her own way she becomes rude and abrupt. And she often sits on the floor with her long legs stretched out in front of her, forcing Yoriko and Kato to step over them each time they want to cross the small room.

Worst of all, she refuses to translate the letters she receives from her father. She says there is nothing in the letters that could possibly interest Yoriko. When Yoriko receives a letter from Bill, Tagenaga reads it aloud and laughs.

Yoriko begs her to teach her English. She believes that if the individual English words in the letters are pointed out to her, she will eventually be able to read them, but Tagenaga gets tired easily and after teaching her a few words per day, she loses interest and asks, 'Why do you want to read his letters? He copies it all from a book. Don't believe everything he tells you. He writes about my mother's illness, but my mother is not ill.'

Her words never fail to upset Yoriko. She resolves to learn to speak English properly now that she has the opportunity to learn it from Tagenaga.

Bill regularly sends small amounts of money, but it is not enough to cover all the expenses needed to support Tagenaga and pay for her tuition as well.

Yoriko sends him a letter telling him that the money is insufficient. He writes back saying that Yoriko must keep an account of the amounts she spends and one day, when they are together, he will refund her.

The aunt warns Yoriko, saying that much unhappiness is caused by two people keeping separate records of the same housekeeping expenditure. When the time comes for the one to ask the other to refund the money, the sum asked always appears to be too much. Money spent on trivialities and titbits can never be accounted for.

Sometimes Tagenaga receives a letter from her mother. Every time this happens she waves it in front of Yoriko, taunting her, 'See, I told you, my father is lying, my mother is not sick. He is lying to you!'

Yoriko comes to the conclusion that Tagenaga does not know that her mother is dying of an incurable disease. What parent would be so cruel as to tell a child such a sadness?

As Tagenaga becomes more accustomed to this life, and feels more at home, she sometimes responds with little gestures of affection and eventually a bonding of sorts takes place between the three people living together in the small house in Tokyo.

When Tagenaga is occupied elsewhere, Yoriko takes her

own letters from Bill, all beginning with the same words, 'My Dearest Yoriko', to the professional letter writer. She never hears anything that could have caused Tagenaga to laugh, and sometimes when she remembers words which Tagenaga had pretended to read from her letters, she asks the letter-writer if he has read every word in the letter. He tells her that he only reads what is in front of him and the words she mentions are not in the letter.

When he finishes reading one of Bill's letters, Yoriko remains at the table and writes her reply immediately. The letter writer transcribes it into English before sending it off.

Days turn into weeks, and weeks into months. Tagenaga is clearly a clever young woman who learns quickly. Her proficiency in Japanese increases by the day and she has a natural aptitude for Ikebana. She progresses quickly, and the teacher conveys her approval to Yoriko.

Her manners also improve. She speaks more softly and gently than when she arrived and she walks slowly, exactly the way that Yoriko has taught her.

After just over a year it is time for Tagenaga to do an exam which will qualify her as a commercial Ikebana artist. She is the first foreigner at this school to pass the exam, which is set in Japanese. Yoriko is bursting with pride that the young woman in her care has done so well.

Yoriko writes to Bill telling him of the great achievement of his daughter. He replies by sending a letter with two air tickets enclosed.

He wants Yoriko to accompany his daughter when she returns to South Africa. He is looking forward to welcoming her in his country. He needs her near him, and they have his wife's blessing that Yoriko can come and help with the housekeeping chores.

As is the custom with the Japanese, Yoriko's family members buy armfuls of presents for Bill and for the sick mother of Tagenaga.

Ellen has mixed feelings about returning home. Her life in Japan is so totally different from her experiences in Johannesburg. Her mother and father would often shout, sometimes even attacking each other with their fists and throwing cups, plates, pots and pans.

And then there is the loneliness. Her mother has an understanding with Bill that she can entertain men in the flat as a way to supplement her income. Whenever her mother is busy entertaining a man, Ellen is locked out of the apartment. She has to keep busy, wandering around the building or the streets until the man has left.

It has been a relief to be out of the flat. She hated the way her mother's guests looked at her. One day her mother told her to stay when four strangers arrived. She gave Ellen some alcohol and the six of them started dancing. The men held her very close.

She vaguely remembers that she and her mother were both naked at some stage and that the men were taking pictures of them. She remembers that she was shy at first, but the more she drank, the less shy she became.

She was surprised when the door opened and she saw her father rushing into the room. She still does not know why he arrived at the flat so unexpectedly. He chased the men out and flung some clothes in her direction before sending her to her room.

There was a lot of screaming as he told her mother that he would kill her if she ever let one of the men touch Ellen. Shortly after this incident, Bill told Ellen that she was to go to study in Japan.

This past year has given her insight into a life where peace and quiet is common. She doesn't want to think about what it will be like to go back to a kitchen piled high with dirty dishes and a mother who doesn't take much notice of her.

With sudden insight she realises that her mother has never cared about her, and might not enjoy having her back. She has been gone for more than a year, and she is scared of what might await her back home.

Kato sees Tagenaga's eyes filling with tears. She walks over to the crying girl and holds her close while rocking to and fro and softly crooning in a singsong voice. Kato is sad but also proud as she remembers how awkward this child had been when she'd arrived at her house. She is still tall and much bigger than herself or Yoriko, but between them they have managed to teach her how to move and how to be quietly graceful. She has indeed turned into a Japanese lady.

On the day of departure, the women shed their tears inside the house. When they appear in public, their emotions have to be in control.

There is a large group of people to see them off at the airport – all Yoriko's family members are there. When they eventually have to move through the departure gate, Yoriko and Ellen bow again and again with solemn dignity. With serene faces they turn away and leave the group of family members behind.

South Africa, 1977

Bill watches the incoming aircraft. He is excited. As far as he can make out from Yoriko's letters, Ellen has turned into a real lady, speaking Japanese fluently as well as being a qualified Ikebana florist: a daughter of which he can be proud. He is looking forward to seeing her. And yes, he also wants to see Yoriko again. Not because he has any special feelings towards her, but because he remembers the care she had taken of him while he was in Japan. It is time to return the favour. In her country she lives in a little cramped house and knows nothing of life. They don't even own cars there. Here he can at least broaden her horizons and show her what life is all about.

He told Dolly that Yoriko was accompanying Ellen only when they were in the car on the way to the airport. She was upset. She did not want to share the flat with another woman. Only when Bill told her that Yoriko would serve as her personal maid and later help in the shop did she relent.

After Bill had posted his letter to Yoriko over a year ago, he gloatingly congratulated himself that he had expertly solved the problem of Ellen and Dolly. Life with Dolly had become difficult even before he'd taken the trip to Tokyo. She was getting more and more demanding, complaining non-stop about the problems she had with Ellen. Bill did not really mind what Dolly did with her life. He spent fewer and fewer nights at the flat, but Dolly would reel him in time and again by leaving so many messages at his office that he'd eventually be forced to go back to the flat to pacify her. She would always demand more and more money, and the small amounts he pilfered from the firm's petty cash account were clearly not enough anymore. He was contemplating how to get Dolly out of his life, but then she was such a hit at swinging parties with the boys in the building trade that he kept on postponing the final break.

He was so sure that he could carry on living an uneventful, quiet life with Mable on the one hand while maintaining a more interesting lifestyle with Dolly. He thought things would remain like this indefinitely – until the day that he found Dolly and Ellen with four men, all naked. What scared him most was that they were taking photographs. He had no intention of getting on the wrong side of the law, and pornographic photographs, with Ellen only thirteen years old, meant trouble of the worst kind. He was beside himself with anger. He broke up the party and sent his daughter to bed.

That was when he started thinking seriously about Ellen's future. If he left her with her mother, she would end up like Dolly. Not all men were as generous and kind-hearted as him and would take a girl off the street and look after her, as he had done with Dolly.

Then, as if a message was sent from some higher source, he read an article singing the praises of the Japanese, and he learnt for the first time that Japanese people enjoy honorary white status in South Africa. This made his head spin, because even though other Asian people, like the Chinese, were considered non-whites in South Africa, as honorary whites, the Japanese had all the advantages of white people in the country.

He thought of Yoriko and the possibility of seeing her again. He wondered how the authorities would be able to distinguish between a Japanese and Chinese person on the street, because he wouldn't be able to. But then he suddenly realised that he had a possible answer to his problem. If the Japanese were considered white, he could save Ellen by sending her to Yoriko. Maybe she could learn Ikebana or how to become a lady.

Although the apartheid system was discriminatory, rich, sophisticated people craved more knowledge from exotic places. He knew that a shop with exotic Ikebana displays and workshops would be a popular and lucrative business in the rich northern suburbs of Johannesburg.

He rushed to the flat to tell Dolly of his plans. While Ellen was in Japan, they could look out for a suitable location to open up the shop. Dolly was excited. Not only would she benefit financially when Ellen returned, but she could get rid of the difficult teenager for more than a year. She immediately agreed to send Ellen to Japan.

As the aircraft nears Johannesburg, Yoriko takes out a letter from her handbag. Her mother had given it to her before she left, and asked Yoriko not to read it before arriving in South Africa. In the letter her mother confirms her deep love for Yoriko and urges her to not feel guilty about the times when Yoriko had reacted with angry words to her mother's advice. She urges her not to be afraid while trying to find her rightful place in life.

Yoriko's emotions run over. She loves her mother as deeply as her mother loves her, and she is sorry that circumstances have forced them to be separated from one another for such a long time. She presses the letter against her heart and knows she will carry these words of love with her forever.

The plane lands. Yoriko looks around her at the people standing in the aisle, putting on their coats, waiting for the steps to be rolled up to the plane for disembarking. She sees herself in the reflection of the window – a small Asian stranger amongst these large men and women of a very different race. She wishes her heart could fold itself into the flat, square warmth of her mother's folded letter.

When Tagenaga arrived in her country, to love her

completely seemed so correct and natural. She was only a child and it was easy for Yoriko and her aunt to comfort her, to teach her and to be gentle and compassionate towards her. Yoriko had seen herself as the mature adult, able to take command and lead. Yet now, amongst these tall people with the many different colours of hair, she feels herself reduced to the status of a child, having to turn to Tagenaga to translate everything that is being said.

As though in a trance, Yoriko moves along the concourse. Then she sees Bill through the glass partition. Shyly, she places a hand on Tagenaga's arm, telling her to look in that direction. The girl reacts instantly by jumping up and down, waving her arms and shouting while Yoriko stands silently, overwhelmed by the emotional magnitude of the moment.

Yoriko maintains a respectful distance and bows discreetly. The first reunion! The tender, more intimate greeting will come later, at home. A secret smile plays lightly around her delicate mouth.

Ellen flings herself at her father, then rushes off towards a rather large blonde, not-so-young woman. 'Mother!' she shouts before flinging her arms around both the man and the woman, drawing them in a circle close around her. The bystanders look at them, smiling, sharing in the special happiness of homecoming.

Yoriko stands a little to one side. Curtly, Bill nods to her before walking towards the exit. At the car, Yoriko sees and hears him speak, but does not fully understand what he says: 'You and your mother sit in the back. Yoriko and I will sit in the front,' Bill directs them while opening the car doors.

One look at Yoriko, and intercepting the glances between her and Bill, Dolly is not prepared to give up the front seat to the stranger. She is not sure what it is, but instinctively she feels threatened by this tiny woman.

'No. Ellen can sit in the back with this girl. I'm sitting in front with you like I always do,' she states.

Yoriko, being the honoured guest and respected companion of his daughter, waits at the front door. But Bill holds the back door open and motions for her to get in at the back.

Ellen gets in next to her.

Yoriko listens to the rapid English spoken by the members of the family. She tries to follow the conversation by looking from the one speaker to the next and attempting to correlate facial expressions and gestures with her own intuition. She concentrates on the sound of the language.

She asks Ellen in Japanese who the blonde woman is. Impatiently, Ellen answers that it is her mother.

Yoriko frowns: 'I do not understand.'

'You do not understand? Boy, how stupid can you be?

How many times have I told you? You would never listen. Don't blame me.'

Yoriko looks at Ellen, bewildered. Ellen, realising that her reply was spiteful, bites her lip. She touches Yoriko's arm in a comforting gesture. Yoriko remembers Ellen's own bewilderment when she arrived in Japan and no one could pronounce her name. That was when Kato had given her the Japanese name of Tagenaga, The Tall One, explaining to her that it was an honour to be given such an unusual name. As time went on, she and Kato were able to instill in Ellen a certain amount of calmness and self-control, and they noticed how the need for her to succumb to fits of anger diminished.

She suddenly feels extremely vulnerable, especially as Ellen seems to have reverted to her rude behaviour. She longs for some kind of assurance from Bill. He is sitting in front of her in the car, but her own cultural customs forbid her to touch him in public.

As they stop in front of a tall building, Bill makes a sweeping movement of his arm. 'This is Hillbrow,' he says. 'And this is where we live.'

Before entering the building, the blonde woman looks at Yoriko and points to the luggage on the pavement that Bill has taken out of the boot of the car.

Yoriko cannot believe that the woman wants her, the

guest, to carry the suitcases, but when Ellen starts taking up a suitcase and urges her in Japanese to do the same, she is left in no doubt. Yoriko is so ashamed of this display of bad manners that she quickly picks up the remaining suitcase and hurries into the foyer, where Bill is holding the door of the lift open for her. They travel up to the tenth floor, where he again holds the door open while she and Ellen carry the suitcases out of the lift.

The three South Africans walk ahead of her along the passage, laughing and talking. She follows them to an open door and enters a big sitting room. Inside the room, she immediately walks over to the huge glass door which opens onto a balcony.

From here she has a magnificent view over a residential area. In the distance she sees green tree-laden hills on which majestic homes proudly proclaim their territorial rights. The swimming pools are flat blue patches of water amongst the trees. The street below is lined with a canopy of huge trees covered in purple flowers. The flowers are everywhere; they lie in a thick carpet along the black street. She has never seen anything so strangely beautiful in her life.

Voices behind her jolt Yoriko back to her immediate surroundings. When Yoriko walks back into the room she sees Bill standing a little apart from the group. She wonders why nobody tells him to sit down and brings him some tea.

Yoriko takes small steps across the room to Bill, tripping along like the Japanese do in their own homes. Ellen and her mother stop talking and look at her. Yoriko appeals to Ellen in Japanese, saying, 'Please ask Bill to sit down. We would love to make him comfortable and bring him tea.'

'What does she want?' Dolly asks suspiciously.

'She says you must sit down.' The daughter looks at her father.

'Who the bloody hell does she think she is to tell anybody what to do in my home?' Dolly explodes. 'Bill, for God's sake! Are you just going to stand there and stare? Since when do we allow the servants to give the orders in this house?'

Bill looks at Yoriko and smiles vacantly. 'Thank you, I don't want to sit down. I must be going. I've a lot to do at the office. I'll see you tonight.' He walks briskly to the front door and departs while Dolly looks at Yoriko disdainfully. Yoriko shuffles over to Ellen. Although the distance between them is not great, the Japanese way of walking takes time.

'Geez!' Dolly says. 'How much work do you think she will be able to do shuffling around like that?'

Yoriko stops in front of Ellen, asking anxiously, 'Why does he go away? You must tell Bill Yoriko says Bill must stay here! Yoriko wants to stay with Bill.' She uses her own name instead of the personal pronoun, as is the custom in Japan.

'You are staying here with us,' Ellen answers offhandedly.

'With you and this other woman?'

'Yes. And she is not "this other woman"; she is my mother.'

'Your birth mother?' Yoriko asks in disbelief.

'Yes, my mother. I've told you a million times!' Ellen says impatiently, as though she is ashamed to be doing all this explaining in Japanese.

'But your mother ... the wife of Bill? Bill wrote that she is very sick. This other woman ...'

'Will you stop calling her "this other woman"?' Ellen feels teary. This makes her shout: 'She's my mother!'

'What's all this arguing about between the two of you?' Dolly looks from the one to the other, irritated because she cannot understand a word.

'She irritates me so when she doesn't understand things,' Ellen replies and wipes away the tears. She looks at her mother and sees the woman whom she knows can make her life a living hell. Trying to turn the situation to her advantage and gain the sympathy of her mother, she says: 'For a whole year she clung to my side, following me around, asking questions, giving me instructions. Do this! Do that! Can you believe it? I was not even allowed to go to the toilet alone! Oh, mother!'

She throws her arms around her mother's neck, and let the tears run freely. 'I missed you and Dad so much!'

Gently Dolly strokes Ellen's hair.

'We also missed you. We are so glad to have you home. And we are so proud of you for getting this diploma. Let's forget all the unpleasantness and concentrate on your future.'

She sits down and pats the settee next to her for Ellen to be seated. 'You know you are very lucky that we allowed you to go to Japan to do this course. Even though you are only sixteen, you can cash in on your training. Bill has decided to buy us a little flower shop. Of course, I will be the manageress, but you will be there full-time.' Dolly's voice rises in excitement. 'You can wear that funny traditional Japanese dress and pretend that you are really Japanese. Oh, the women will think you are so special if you speak Japanese as well. You can also teach rich women all about Japanese flower arranging. Isn't that marvellous?'

Dolly smiles at Ellen, waiting for a response, but Ellen only stares at her. She has just arrived in the country, and she already has to start working. Does her mother not understand that she would like to spend some time with her?

Her mother continues, 'I can even start a high-class escort agency like Bill says they have in Tokyo. She giggles conspiratorially. Her eyes gleam excitedly while she continues to discuss the details with Ellen. 'We are going to have cards printed with good-luck Japanese characters on them. We will send them to some of the prominent businessmen in town together with a nice little Ikebana arrangement in a tiny vase to stand on their desk. Bill and I have thought about everything while you were away. We will make lots of money. Won't that be nice?'

Yoriko has been looking anxiously from the one to the other. Noticing Dolly smiling, she stands with her hands together and smiles as well, anxious to be accepted by this woman-mother whom, it seems, is no longer ill. But Dolly gets up from the settee and gives Yoriko a sidelong glance before walking out of the room and saying to Ellen, 'Tell her to take your stuff to our room and start unpacking.'

'What does she say?' Yoriko asks Ellen.

'Oh, she goes on about stuff. Help me, will you? Let's take my things to the room.' Ellen picks up her bag and gestures to Yoriko to bring her suitcases.

When Yoriko enters the bedroom Ellen is sitting on one of the twin beds while her mother is lying on the other with her eyes shut. Dolly tries to figure out what it is about this 'Oriental' that makes her lungs constrict and her heart beat faster. She tries to understand why Bill brought this woman to South Africa. Her head is pounding with an oncoming migraine. He said this woman would be their servant, but why does she not act like one? Why is Ellen so taken up with her?

Quietly Yoriko puts the luggage down and asks in a whisper, 'Where is my room?'

'Put your suitcase up against the wall over there,' Ellen points to a corner.

'Where do I sleep?' Yoriko asks. 'Here?' and she points to the mat between the two beds.

'No,' Ellen whispers, 'this is our room.' She looks at Yoriko and tries to explain kindly, 'My mother and I sleep here. You will have to sleep in the passage, or in the sitting room. I am sorry.'

'These are strange words coming from the mouth of my little sister, Tagenaga.'

Ellen gets up from the bed and whispers: 'I didn't think you would mind. I had to sleep on the floor in your country; I thought you were used to it. Besides, you won't like a bed, so why are you complaining?'

'Come,' Yoriko says to Ellen, taking her by the hand and leading her out of the room. In the sitting room she stands facing Ellen, an authoritative figure in the middle of the room. She gestures to Ellen to come closer, then sinks down onto her knees, while Ellen does the same, adopting the traditional Japanese sitting posture a mother takes up opposite a child she wants to instruct in some serious manner.

Yoriko bows her head until it touches the floor and says, 'I greet my little sister, Tagenaga, in this wonderful country, with words that are inadequate and entirely unworthy to convey my sincere gratitude to you for your acceptance of me as your guest in your wonderful home.'

She lifts her head, and looks at Ellen, smiling, 'It is our custom when we enter the home of a respected and honoured friend to bring gifts to all the members of the family. Yet I am at a loss to know how to address the honourable woman you call mother. Please explain.'

Ellen does not look at Yoriko and says, 'I don't know what to explain.'

Yoriko smiles, saying, 'Yoriko hears the name of The Tall One, so difficult for us to say, but now Yoriko respectfully accepts this name "Ellen" belonging to my little sister in her wonderful country. Please explain the miracle that caused your sick mother to recover so miraculously.' She looks at Ellen curiously.

Ellen keeps her head down while answering. 'If you want to know when she was ill, you must ask my father. I know nothing of that. They sent me away.'

Accepting this answer, Yoriko gets up and fetches a large parcel she had taken great care of in the aircraft during the long flight from Tokyo to Johannesburg. Going down onto her knees in one graceful movement of her body, she places the parcel in front of Ellen, smiling.

Ellen unwraps it, and lifts the lid off the box. She removes the tissue paper and, handling it gently, reveals an exquisitely carved wooden shrine. 'Thank you, Yoriko, it is beautiful.' She accepts the present with awe. 'It will always remind me of the time I spent with you.'

Swaying upright onto her feet with a smooth backward rolling movement of her body, she lifts the wooden shrine and carefully places it on top of the cocktail cabinet. She walks back to where Yoriko is sitting and once again sinks down onto her knees opposite the Japanese woman.

'Yoriko, you must realise that we are not in Tokyo any longer. Here women are free, and they do what they like, and they go where they like. I cannot be with you all day long. My mother was telling me about this flower shop they have bought for me. I'll be giving lessons there and doing flower arrangements. I'll be very busy.'

Yoriko smiles and answers with genuine enthusiasm: 'That is good news and my heart sings for my little sister. It will be my pleasure, my little sister, to be at your side and support you in your shop.'

Her voice faltering, Ellen answers: 'You do not understand.

You cannot be at my side.' Noticing Yoriko's hurt expression, she hurries on. 'It is not that I do not want you in the shop, but it will be embarrassing for us if people find out that you are staying with us.'

'Yoriko does not understand.' She frowns, looking at Ellen.

'It's very difficult to explain. I really do not mind, but the people who make the laws here do not want people from the Orient to stay with white people.'

Yoriko lifts her eyebrows, registering surprise.

'This does not count for the Japanese, but people do not know that. Oh, don't pretend you didn't know! Now that we are here, we just have to do what they say. I did not make these silly old laws. There are laws which make it illegal for non-whites and whites to live together. In this country you are not white, because you look like an Asian and Asians are black. My parents can be jailed for your presence in our home. For you to become white, we have to prove you are Japanese every time we step out. My father says it would be better for you to stay indoors until we know how this honorary thing with Japanese people works.'

Yoriko thinks about what Ellen has just told her. 'No. Yoriko does not understand,' she says.

Ellen had not expected that it would be left to her to explain the laws about race to Yoriko. Especially as she does not fully understand the implications herself. She blinks her eyes, looking at Yoriko, and remembers how happy she had been in Japan. How is she going to explain Bill's direct orders that Yoriko should not be seen with them in public? Then she thinks about the privileged life Yoriko had in Japan as a member of one of the respected families in a very high-class neighbourhood. There she had also encountered many incidents of class distinction and social segregation. Grasping at the only explanation she can think of, she blurts out: 'I am so sorry, but you are low-class here.'

Yoriko's eyes glint dangerously. 'You,' she whispers, 'you say Yoriko … Yoriko is low-class?'

She lifts her head in a gesture of absolute conviction and undisputed awareness of her own social standing.

Ellen is completely out of her depth, unsure how to restore the mutual trust that has existed between them. Her lack of general knowledge and inadequate education leave her speechless, but the rigid training and cultural guidance she had been subjected to in Japan force her not to lift her eyes off the ground. And by looking up she might reveal to Yoriko her ignorance and discomfort.

At this moment Dolly comes into the room, sees the two women kneeling opposite each other, and notices the regal bearing of the small foreigner sitting back on her heels with her spine stiff and rigid and her head high.

'Ellen!' she snaps. Ellen jumps to her feet, thankful that her mother has broken up this unpleasant deadlock, and feels herself blushing. Sullenly, she acknowledges her mother's right to know what they are talking about.

'Yoriko doesn't understand the objections we have against coloured people in this country.'

'Why not?' Dolly is astonished. Looks at Yoriko critically and says, 'I mean, look at her! Everything about her is different. I'm not one for politics, but you can't blame the government for making laws. Heaven knows. But I'm not having her here staying with us and throwing her weight around, as though she's one of us. And you'd better make that quite clear to her right now.' She rubs her forehead and wishes the headache would subside. Then she adds: 'Tell her she is jolly lucky we allow her to sleep here with us in the flat. We owe her nothing. Bill paid her a lot of money for your studies. And now she wants a better life from us. Actually she should be sleeping in the servant quarters on the roof. Don't be sorry for her, tell her that!'

'Well, what do you think I've been doing?' Ellen retorts petulantly. 'You don't listen to a word I'm saying!' Ellen feels her stomach dropping. She is truly glad to see her mother again, but it is clear that they have reverted to the same level of anger and frustration that has existed between them ever since she can remember. It feels as if she has never been away.

Dolly walks over to Yoriko and points a finger at her. 'You mustn't think you can come over here and put on airs. You're nothing but a servant.' She takes a step closer to Yoriko, now pointing a finger at Ellen, and hisses, 'And do you hear how she speaks to her mother after staying with you for all this time? That doesn't say much for your high-class manners, does it?'

'Cut it out!' Ellen cries. 'She can't understand a word you're saying.'

'Why don't you tell her in her own bloody language, seeing as you're so clever?'

'I will, if you give me a chance,' Ellen replies insolently. She turns to Yoriko and speaks rapidly in Japanese. 'My mother says if you want to know what class you are, then it is what we call servant class.'

Yoriko gets up onto her feet, and slowly and distinctly says: 'Yoriko is not a servant.'

'Look,' Ellen says, 'I did not make these laws. Here we have white and black people and the blacks have always been the servants.'

Not understanding a word being said, Dolly interrupts the conversation. 'Tell her to go to the kitchen and make tea.'

Ellen glares at her mother, lifts her shoulders, and snarls: 'Here you go again! You ask her yourself. I am not going to be your translator.'

Dolly walks up to Yoriko, nudges her arm and gestures with her thumb over her shoulder towards the kitchen: 'Get going!'

Yoriko's mouth tightens firmly and her slanting eyes open wide, but she does not move. Dolly sees yellow spots around her. Her head is exploding and this woman is the cause of it all. She pushes her in the direction of the kitchen.

'I said get into the kitchen, you nitwit!'

Frightened, Yoriko flings her arms into the air, crying in a high-pitched voice for Ellen to help her. Dolly pushes her hard and screams: 'Stop the hysterics!'

With a mournful wail Yoriko sinks down onto the floor, covering her face with her hands, sobbing loudly. Ellen stands rooted to the spot, fascinated, unsure of herself yet not wanting to be personally involved. She scrambles out of the room to the bedroom, where she starts unpacking her suitcase.

After a while Dolly walks into the room. 'I told your father it was a bloody stupid idea letting this woman bring you home, but he wouldn't listen. Now I'm the one who has to put up with all this shit.' She pauses for a moment. 'I can't understand why he did it. She's not even strong and I can't see how she can work properly. She is not going to stay here wailing like an animal. What she needs is a bloody good hiding.'

She looks at Ellen closely. 'Now don't you go and spoil her while she's here. You had to be friendly while you were studying in Japan, but now you are home it's quite different. You must realise we are doing her a favour putting her up like this. Letting her live with us isn't legal.' She sighs again. 'Bloody Bill has a bloody nerve to do this to me. I'll tell him straight when I see him tonight.'

They hear the front door open and close. 'If that's him now, I'll go and speak to him right away.' Ellen follows her mother out of the room, just in time to see Yoriko disappearing into the sitting room with a fluttering of hands, and the pitiful sound of sobbing.

'Oh, my God!' Dolly rolls her eyes heavenward, and hurries to the sitting room with Ellen close on her heels. They find Yoriko kneeling on the floor in front of Bill, who looks most uncomfortable standing in the middle of the room. She has clasped the bottom of his jacket with both hands and is beseeching him with a disconcerting flow of words. He frowns at Dolly and Ellen, saying, 'What the hell is wrong with this girl?'

When nobody answers, he bends down, lifts Yoriko to her feet, and helps her over to the settee. She clings onto his hairy wrist, with both her petal-white hands, making no attempt to control her sobbing.

'I told you this would cause trouble,' Dolly nods at Yoriko.

'What did she do?' he asks. 'What happened?'

'Put on airs,' Dolly continues tritely, then adds in a querulous tone of voice, 'I don't know why you did it. I can keep her busy cleaning the flat, and doing little things for us, but apparently that doesn't suit the madam. She says she's not a servant. I want to know about this woman, I am not stupid, I want to know.'

'She's an artist, Mother,' Ellen interjects.

'Now that you have spent a whole year studying in Tokyo the last thing we need is another artist. I've already hired three servant girls to help you in the shop; there is no place for an artist or another servant.'

Bill looks at Yoriko sitting forlornly at his side on the settee. He takes a handkerchief out of his coat pocket and hands it to her. He realises that five years have passed since he saw her in Japan. She has aged and although he knew she was small, she now appears too tiny, even insignificant in this large room. Dolly is right, he thinks. She is not even pretty. I should never have brought her here with Ellen. The best thing would be to keep her busy working in the flat until he can work out what to do with her. His mind is racing. If he leaves Dolly in charge, she might make it so uncomfortable for Yoriko that she might decide to take the first flight back to Japan. He cannot remember when last Dolly had a servant that stayed for longer than three weeks in her service. Some even leave without waiting for their pay.

How foolish he was to have brought Yoriko to South Africa; how foolish to have written to her at all.

Bill remembers writing to Yoriko after he saw an article on Japanese love letters in a glossy magazine. He was waiting for a haircut at his barber when he found the magazine. The beautiful photographs of cherry blossoms in Japan reminded him of Yoriko. On impulse, he decided to copy the style of these letters. He tore the pages out of the magazine and stuffed them into his pocket. Later, in his tin-shanty office on the building site of his firm's latest housing development, he took the article out of his pocket and flattened the pages on his desk. He was fascinated with the poetic Eastern style of writing quoted in the article. Experimenting with this ambiguous and, to him, very feminine way of writing, and recalling Yoriko's naïve enjoyment of his pen sketches, he wrote her a flamboyant letter just to see what would happen. When he received an answer from her in exactly the same quaint style, it flattered his ego and amused him to write to her occasionally in the same manner. He looks at her now, hunched pathetically at the settee. She addresses him in Japanese. 'Bill, Yoriko does not understand. Too many things have happened today.' Bill looks at Ellen to translate, but Dolly interjects.

'Why does she keep saying "Yoriko, Yoriko"?' Dolly asks impatiently.

'That's just their way of talking,' Ellen replies, pleased to be able to show off some of her knowledge. 'They consider it very bad manners to say "I". They believe it may give the person they are talking to the idea that they are acting superior and giving orders.'

Then Dolly notices the carved wooden shrine on top of the cocktail cabinet. 'That's an interesting little thing. Did you bring it back with you, Ellen?'

'No. It is a present from Yoriko.'

'It will look very nice in the flower shop. We must remember to take it along tomorrow.'

Yoriko, having followed this conversation with her eyes, gets up gracefully and leaves the room.

Dolly points to her retreating back, laughing. 'She won't get very far, trying to walk down to the shops like that. It will take her all day.' Anger flares up again. 'Bill, where the hell do you think she will find the time to do all the work around the flat if she persists in shuffling along like that? The first thing we will have to do is get her a servant's uniform. That will enable her to move more freely.' He knows she is testing him, waiting for him to come to Yoriko's defence. Anything that can confirm her suspicion.

Yoriko comes back with her arms laden with parcels. Dropping down on her knees, she spreads them out on the floor in front of her. She has presents for everybody, and now she tries desperately to give everybody a new chance to fix this situation that has gone all wrong.

'Bill,' Ellen calls across the room to her father. Yoriko lifts an eyebrow, hearing the familiar way Ellen addresses her father. 'Tell her about you and Mother. I do not know what she wants to know, but ever since we got off the plane she's been nagging me to explain things to her.'

'She won't understand a word I am saying,' Bill replies.

'Of course she will!' Dolly explodes. 'She understood you well enough when you were over there, didn't she?'

'That was years ago. Besides, that was different.'

'You bet that was different,' Dolly smirks. 'As I keep saying to you, lover boy, on your own, your life's your own, but in my house you keep your bloody hands off my servants. I can see I'll have enough problems with her without you being around. As a matter of fact, the more I see of her, the less I like the idea of having her around all the time. She's not at all like our blacks. She gives me the creeps.'

'You know just as well as I do that I can't afford to take her anywhere else, and that is all there is to it,' Bill replies acidly.

Dolly storms out of the sitting room and into the bedroom, slamming the door.

Yoriko looks at Bill, but neither he nor Ellen take the slightest notice of her. They continue talking.

'Didn't you tell her about Dolly and me?' he asks.

'No. Why would I have? You were the one who kept on writing to her.' Ellen looks embarrassed, gets up, and follows Dolly into the bedroom.

Yoriko immediately slides off the settee onto the floor, where she kneels in front of Bill and looks at him imploringly. He notices the dark rings around her eyes and feels a tiny sensation of guilt trickling down his spine. 'You must be tired after the long trip.'

She looks up at him. 'Yoriko speak English.'

'I'm pleased to hear that. We won't need an interpreter, then. That should make things easier.'

'This woman,' she points towards the bedroom. 'Yoriko not happy. Bad woman.'

'You mustn't say that, she's Ellen's mother. And let me give you a word of advice. Please behave yourself while you are staying here with her. She's doing you a great favour and you better realise that.'

'No! She no-class woman!'

Yoriko had promised herself that she would speak slowly when she communicated with English speakers. But in the excitement of the moment the few words she knows tumble from her lips and Bill misunderstands her.

'Of course she's not a cross woman! She's not a cross woman at all, even though she does swear quite a bit. She's a very nice woman, that's why she's Ellen's mother.' He leans back with a self-satisfied smile as though he does not need to say another word, and he pinches her lightly on the cheek.

She grabs hold of his wrist with both hands and fondles her face against the back of his hand. She looks up at him eagerly, as though his words have just penetrated her mind. 'Of course Bill agree! She no-class woman! Why Bill take no-class woman to be mother of his child?'

He looks at her without paying much attention. She jerks his hand, and asks loudly, 'Why? Why? Tell Yoriko! Why Bill not have good woman for wife? This woman bad. Bad!'

'I've got a wonderful woman for a wife.'

A light goes on for him.

'Of course, Ellen does not know my wife. She is rich, high-class, and the doctors and nurses cost me so much money. All these years, she was too sick to have children, and I do not know how I would have gone on living if it was not for Dolly and Ellen.'

'This bad woman not wife?' Yoriko asks.

He smiles at her as though he is letting her into a secret. 'No. Dolly is not my wife.'

'She concubine?'

He laughs out loud. 'Yes, all right. We can say she is a concubine.'

Yoriko's eyes flash furiously. 'Yoriko not stay in house with concubine! Yoriko high-class! Yoriko not stay!'

He is amused at her outburst of anger and speaks to her in a soothing voice, remembering how he had anticipated having a good time with her. She has changed in the past five years, but Bill is sure he can work his way around that.

'You're a little devil, aren't you? So you think you are not a concubine?' He tries to pull her onto the settee beside him, but she resists. She gets up, glaring at him.

He stands up, straightens his jacket and looks at her accusingly. 'So that's how you want to play it: hard to get! I suppose you think I'll run after you. I know you must be tired after the long flight. Just remember, you're staying here with us. Adapt to our way of living, and we will all be happy.'

Yoriko looks at him and angrily explodes 'Yoriko not happy!'

This outburst takes him by surprise, and he moves a few steps backwards trying to get away from her, but she rushes at him, pummelling his body with ineffectual blows. He grabs hold of her wrists and shakes her. She throws her head back and wails. Still writhing in his grip, she twists and turns her body, sobbing hysterically. He pushes her away and for the second time on that very first day on African soil, she collapses into a little heap on the floor. Covering her head with her arms, she lies sobbing, face down on the carpet.

Ellen and Dolly rush into the room. He gives them a look of utter disgust, walks out of the flat, and slams the front door behind him.

The next morning Yoriko is calm and composed. During the night she had prayed to her ancestor Oyo, and rereading her mother's letter, she gains strength from the words.

She does not doubt that Oyo will answer her prayers. He was directly responsible for her becoming a painter and it was because of her painting skills that she had met Bill and fallen in love with him. He will sort out this terrible situation for her.

She calmly gets up when she hears the other two women waking. She remains serene even when she is ordered to make breakfast.

She hears Dolly calling because Ellen is struggling to put

on her beautiful kimono all by herself. She immediately starts to help Ellen. She is in a hurry, because she wants to dress in her own kimono to accompany Ellen to the opening ceremony of the flower shop. Ellen had told her before that she would not be welcome in the shop. But surely Ellen had been wrong. How could she not be at the opening after she had helped the girl to become an arranger of flowers?

When Bill walks into the flat, Yoriko's heart contracts involuntarily. She is incredibly confused, but she knows Oyo will answer her prayers. She does not like the fact that Bill has a concubine. But she will accept this fact, like wives in Japan accept that their husbands may have a few women who are allowed to lay claim to his time. However, she will make it clear to Bill that she cannot share a house with a concubine who treats her like a servant.

At home in Japan she is sure of herself. She knows where she fits into the social structure but here it is different.

Bill is smiling. 'Guess what?' he says. 'The newspaper called to say they will send a photographer and a journalist to the shop. But only a bit later after everybody has arrived. We have invited so many.'

'Isn't that wonderful, Ellen?' Dolly gushes excitedly. 'Aren't you thrilled that you are going to be famous? You have so much to be thankful for. My parents never did a thing for me when I was your age.'

They get up and Yoriko tightens the broad sash just blow Ellen's chest. She also adjusts the bow at the back.

Ellen thanks her and starts to gather her handbag, urging Dolly and Bill to hurry. She does not want to be late for her own opening.

Yoriko calls anxiously to Ellen in her own language, 'Wait! Wait! I'm not quite ready yet. I still have to put on my kimono.'

Ellen sighs and says, 'I have told you, you're not coming with us.'

Momentarily bewildered, Yoriko stands quite still. As Dolly passes her on her way to the front door, she says to Yoriko, 'When you've cleaned the flat this morning, you can finish unpacking Ellen's clothes. Those that are very dirty can be washed, the other things just need to be pressed. The iron is in the cupboard in the kitchen.'

'Oh, Ma!' Ellen interrupts. 'Stop wasting your breath, you speak too fast, she can't understand a word you're saying.'

'My God, yes!' Dolly says in exasperation. 'I've forgotten the bloody girl is uneducated. Imagine anybody not learning to speak proper English?' She looks at Yoriko with her hands on her hips, 'What am I going to do with you?' Then she snaps her fingers at Ellen: 'Translate, I don't want to be late.'

Ellen feels like crying; she cannot look Yoriko in the eye. Bill sees this and puts his hand on her shoulder. 'Come girl,' he says, turning her away from Yoriko, 'you have a shop to open.' He also avoids Yoriko's eyes.

They walk out of the flat and Yoriko starts crying. What has happened to the happy, intimate understanding that existed between her and Bill in their letters? And between her and Tagenaga? They have been constantly together for the past twenty months; every minute of the day the one knew where the other one was. Yesterday she would have replied yes to anybody who'd asked whether she knew this girl. She would have said that she is her friend. No, she would have said that Tagenaga is more than a friend. She is her little sister. There are no secrets between them and the relationship brings joy and happiness to her heart.

The girl who has just left the flat is a stranger.

Yoriko tries to control her emotions but the tears are streaming down her cheeks and the pain in her heart overwhelms her. She collapses into her bedding on the floor. She eventually falls asleep and only wakes up when loud laughter and noise fill the flat.

Ellen comes rushing in.

'Yoriko, wake up! Yoriko! We've had a wonderful day! We were taken to lunch by such posh people. And lots of women are coming to take lessons from me. They were impressed because I'm so young. But I remembered everything you told me: "The teacher is very important!" Remember you told me that? And the teacher speaks only when there is complete silence. It was so easy, just like you said it would be. I thought about you, and I wasn't frightened at all. Isn't it wonderful?'

She takes Yoriko's hands and pulls her to her feet. 'I'm so happy. They took lots of photographs, and I'm going to make pots of money and be really rich. Now you can come and help me get out of this kimono. I don't know if I'm going to wear this often, it's much too tight, and I'm so hot I could die.'

Dolly walks into the sitting room and opens the curtains to let the sunlight in, saying, 'Ellen, you'd better tell this bloody girl she cannot lie around sleeping all bloody day. She'd better hurry and get this flat cleaned up. If she wants to sleep in the passage, she has to get up and see that it is all cleared away before we wake up. The place looks like a bloody pig sty.'

Yoriko's thoughts are in a muddle. While she washes the dishes she tries to reconstruct and evaluate her situation. She has been in the country for only a day, but it feels like a lifetime. She needs to talk to somebody. Somebody from the Japanese embassy, whom she can speak to in her own language. There are many things she has to know.

Then there is the matter of the English language. She has

looked up the word 'bloody' in her dictionary. She could not find a definition that could possibly apply to all the instances in which the word is used in this house. Bloody girl. Bloody work. Bloody flat.

Early the next morning after Ellen and her mother have left the flat, Yoriko quickly tidies up the place, then she takes her passport, locks up, and leaves the building. She wants to get a taxi to the Japanese Embassy. Very soon she arrives at the main street, where she walks along admiring the beautiful shops and display windows.

She stops for a moment, undecided as to which direction to take. Then she sees right in front of her a woman sitting in a small glass cage built into the wall of the building. Above the cubicle is written the word 'Information'.

'Please, I'm sorry.' She attracts the woman's attention. 'Please, Japanese Embassy?'

'Yes. How many tickets do you want?' the woman asks.

'Tickets?' Yoriko asks.

'Yes. How many tickets do you want?' the woman repeats. Then noticing Yoriko's puzzled expression she asks kindly, 'Is it for yourself?'

'Yes, please.' Yoriko nods her head in eager agreement.

'What price?'

Yoriko frowns, and turns her ear towards the woman, much as a deaf person would. The woman looks as Yoriko, then beckons her to come around to the side of the cubicle where she points to a drawing of a seating arrangement and says, 'This is the Embassy Theatre and these are the seats. What price do you want?'

Yoriko immediately realises that there has been a misunderstanding. 'No theatre,' she says, shaking her head emphatically. She takes out her passport and repeats the word 'embassy'.

'Oh, embassy!' the woman laughs, and takes Yoriko's passport and pages through it, noticing that it is very new. She says, 'I don't know where you must go. But just around the corner there is a police station. We have many immigrants in this part of the city, and I am sure the police will be able to help you.'

Yoriko shakes her head. 'No police!'

'They are very kind and helpful,' the woman reassures Yoriko. However, seeing how crestfallen Yoriko looks, she apologises. 'I'm sorry I don't know what else to suggest. Perhaps you could go to the bank across the road. They might help you.'

Yoriko takes an immediate liking to the girl at the bank. This is just how Tagenaga looked when she arrived in Japan.

A rush of homesickness overwhelms Yoriko. She holds out her passport to the girl and repeats the word 'embassy'.

The girl glances through the passport, then smiles at Yoriko and shakes her head.

'I'm sorry, there is no Japanese embassy in this country, but the police have a special branch handling the affairs of immigrants.' She notices Yoriko's hesitancy and asks, 'What is it you want to know?' Yoriko wonders how she can explain her predicament to this girl.

There are so many things she wants to know. First of all, she wants to find somebody with whom she can speak in Japanese, somebody of culture and good manners who she could ask: 'How is it possible that Bill Bosch, when he came to my country, could act like a true-born, high-class gentleman, and now, when Yoriko is visiting him in his own country, he allows his family to treat Yoriko like a servant? How is it possible that he can ask Yoriko in a letter to lend money to his daughter in Japan and then, when he meets Yoriko for the first time in his country, not even find time to greet Yoriko properly, let alone thank Yoriko for lending his daughter money!' Perhaps he is staying away from her like a criminal who is ashamed to acknowledge his money debts? She finds these things very strange.

The girl, noticing Yoriko's uncertain manner, comes to a

sudden conclusion: This woman needs help. 'Come,' she says, taking Yoriko by the hand and leading her out of the building. 'I'll take you to the police station. They will be able to help you.'

As Yoriko is being led along, she resigns herself to the inevitable, realising that she has to start somewhere if she wants to get any answers. This means that she has to accept the consequences of the decision made by this charming girl.

The beautiful young girl escorts Yoriko to the police station, where she converses in a most friendly manner with the men on duty. They laugh pleasantly together. She hands over Yoriko's passport and then she takes leave of Yoriko, kindly wishing her a happy day.

The policeman pages through her passport and shakes his head at her. Yoriko's face is completely expressionless as she stares back at him. He asks her where she is staying, and she hands him a card Bill had given her, on which the address and the phone number of the flat is written. He dials the number, speaks and then puts down the receiver. He hands her back her passport and tells her to wait. She sits down quietly, making herself as inconspicuous as possible, not knowing what to expect next.

About half an hour later, Bill enters the police station with a wide smile. After speaking with the policemen behind the counter for a few minutes, he takes her by the arm and they walk out of the building together. His smile disappears as they get outside. He holds onto her arm until they get into his car, then looks at her, frowning furiously. He does not say a single word until they get back to the block of flats.

'What were you doing at the police station?' he asks as he gets into the lift. She does not answer. When they get to the door of the flat, he holds out his hand. 'Give me the key.'

He unlocks the door and they walk into the sitting room.

She looks at him fearfully. Then she drops onto her knees and sits back onto her heels, holding her hands clasped in front of her. 'Please, Bill. Many things Yoriko not understand.'

He takes a seat and looks at her speculatively, his anger evaporating. 'Well, if there are things you do not understand, ask me. Do not go to the police. You were extremely lucky today that I happened to be in the flat when they phoned.'

Realising that he is no longer angry, she asks: 'Bill want some tea?'

'No, pour me some brandy.'

When she has him comfortably settled with a glass of brandy in his hand, he looks so benevolent that she decides, in spite of her very limited knowledge of English, to try to ask him all the questions for which she cannot find answers in her own mind.

After listening to her broken sentences and miming gestures he realises that he probably owes her an explanation. He says he is sorry about the misunderstanding as he had not realised that she thought Ellen's mother and his sick wife were the same person. But now that she is here, she must be able to see how difficult things are for him. He expects her to behave and not complicate matters for him by being unreasonable.

'Dolly is a good woman and there is no need for you to get upset about her,' he says forcefully.

He tells her that as he can never divorce his wife, because of her illness, he cannot marry Dolly. 'When I met you in Japan, you made me forget all the worries I had here. I admired your elegance' he said. 'You are so feminine and I thought you could teach Ellen to be like you.

Yoriko concentrates on his words and tries to understand every sentence.

'If I had never met you, I don't know what would have become of Ellen.' He speaks slowly and looks Yoriko straight in the eyes. 'When I wrote to you to ask you to teach Ellen your ways, you could have refused my offer. Remember, she was a paying guest. Now I am returning the favour. You are a guest, but you are not paying.'

Yoriko tells him that she does not understand why he wrote her a letter with the intimate salutation 'My Dearest Yoriko'.

'Because you are a wonderful person, and I liked you the moment I saw you. I immediately realised that you are a gifted painter and a clever woman.'

Bill leans forward towards Yoriko, takes both her hands in his, and looks into her eyes. 'I was convinced of your true spirit when I made love to you, and you remained forever in my heart. I do not want you to spoil this time that we will have together by being silly. I thought you would be grateful to have the opportunity to look after Ellen and to be a part of getting her adjusted to life, by supervising her studies. She will one day give you all the necessary credit.'

'Now Bill true speak!' Yoriko replies animatedly. 'Yoriko good woman. Yoriko much love Ellen, like a sister. Dolly no good woman. She speak like no-class woman. Together we take Ellen and stay high-class hotel. Much better.'

'That's impossible. I can't take Ellen away from Dolly. She is her mother.'

'That one mistake! Bill now see Yoriko, no mistake, wonderful person! Yoriko live in this country, look after Ellen, make many beautiful flower arrangements. Bill, Yoriko and Ellen become very happy family.' She looks at him with excitement shining in her eyes. 'Bill write Yoriko wonderful promise-you letter, saying: "Yoriko teach Ellen Ikebana, then Ellen and Yoriko come South Africa together and Bill fix everything." Yoriko now waiting.'

'That's right,' Bill replies. 'And I went to a hell of a lot of trouble to get a visa for you, to allow you to stay here for three months. It is not my fault that the laws of the country insisted that you have a return ticket before they would grant you a visa. Three months is a long time and you can live happily here with us. You can get to know the city and see how different our lifestyle is compared to yours. Dolly and Ellen will be working during the day and if you are sensible you and I can have some exciting times together.'

In his own mind, Bill had resolved all the problems. 'I cannot take you to a high-class hotel as you suggest, because they won't allow you into the hotel.' Bill sighs and continues: 'According to the laws of this country, you are not white, and for that reason you are not welcome in South Africa.'

Yoriko looks at him incredulously, and he quickly amends that statement by saying, 'Of course, I do not agree with that at all, but I do not make the laws. However, we all have to obey the laws of the country.'

Yoriko looks at him intently before saying. 'Yoriko high-class but not accepted in this country, but Dolly, no-class woman can call Yoriko no-class. Not understand.'

Suddenly Bill loses his patience and raises his voice, 'For Christ's sake! I can't go on repeating myself. Don't you see, it's because you are Japanese!' Yoriko gives him an icy stare.

'Yoriko think Bill not high-class person. Bill just pretend-man in my country.' She lifts her head haughtily, looking at him with cool deliberation.

Not quite sure of the meaning of this disconcerting statement, he gets up and walks across the room, walks back and stands in front of Yoriko, looking down at her. 'It's no good trying to explain it to you. You will never understand. Either you accept the facts or you don't. But I am not going to discuss this matter any further with you, you understand. I don't want you to mention it again.' He sits down and takes her hands in his.

His voice becomes intimate. 'You must be reasonable. We could have been enjoying ourselves instead of sitting here talking. Yoriko, I came here this morning looking for you, to greet you privately, and to enjoy the pleasure of your company. We have not been alone since you arrived, and what I have to say to you is not for the ears of other people. I was most surprised when you were not here. Why did you go to the police? What is there that they can do for you that I cannot do?'

'Yoriko look for Japanese embassy.'

He frowns. If she really manages to get hold of somebody who speaks her language and she starts talking, they could sell this story as sensational news to any one of the newspapers. If she mentions Bill's name, it won't take them long to put two and two together and link Ellen and the flower shop to this whole affair, and that could do him a lot of harm. Especially if she starts telling them about the way Dolly insists on treating her as a servant! That would be front-page news all over the world, and probably do irreparable damage to his private life as well as his credibility at work.

Through his position at the construction firm and his Afrikaans connections in government, Bill has been able to arrange many building concessions. But it necessitates that he keeps a low profile. He will have to make sure that she does not get another opportunity like this morning's.

He pulls her towards him. 'Yoriko, you must promise me that you will never go out of the flat alone again. We will take you wherever you want to go. But you have to stay in the flat during the day. I do not know exactly when it will be, but I will come, and we will enjoy each other's company. I will also teach you English. You would like that, wouldn't you?'

'Thank you Bill. Yoriko wants to learn English. It is very important.'

'And at the weekends, Ellen and I will take you out into the country to paint pictures.'

'Yoriko must paint every day. Yoriko must travel many

places, look at this wonderful country, take many photographs. When Yoriko return to Tokyo, Yoriko must have many beautiful pictures to explain this very wonderful country – not dream-of-my-heart place!'

But he isn't listening to her stilted speech any longer. He is wondering how to ensure that she stays in the flat. When he suddenly finds his answer, he looks up excitedly.

'Yoriko, bring your inks and paper, and we will go to the botanical gardens. You will be able to paint there all afternoon and we can have some tea in the restaurant.'

Yoriko is soon ready and they leave the flat. He drives slowly, asking her often if she would like him to stop so that she can take photographs. He stops in front of a row of shops, telling her to wait while he buys cigarettes and a newspaper. He also enters a hardware shop and buys a Yale lock. One that can be opened from one side only.

They spend a leisurely afternoon in the botanical gardens. Every now and then she shows him what she has painted. He reads the newspaper and relaxes, enjoying this outing more than he cares to admit.

While they are drinking tea in the restaurant, an elderly woman sitting at a table next to them starts speaking to Yoriko, telling her that she has visited Japan a few times and loved each moment. She patiently phrases her words and between the two of them they manage to have quite a lengthy conversation. Yoriko is captivated by the woman's cameo brooch with the beautifully carved white bust of a woman set against a blue background. The woman tells Yoriko she inherited it from her grandmother and that it has been handed down through the generations of her family for many years.

Seeing how excited the cameo has made her, Bill picks up a sheet of paper lying on the table and starts sketching in pencil. She hands him the ink and he carefully dips a brush. When he is finished he hands the little painting to Yoriko. She immediately recognises the profile of her own face. Her delicate features are set in an oval frame. It is uncannily like the picture of the cameo she has admired.

'An African cameo,' he says.

Yoriko laughs delightedly and puts her hands together. 'Bill wonderful artist. Yoriko thank Bill very much.'

It is quite dark when they get back to the flat.

Yoriko does not want to spend time in Dolly's presence and she quickly rolls out her blankets. When he is sure Yoriko is asleep, Bill fixes the Yale lock to the outside of the front door.

The next morning when Dolly and Ellen open the door to

leave, Yoriko, standing close by, immediately notices the lock. When she hears the extra click, it takes her only a second to realise the significance of this sound.

Even though she knows better, she tries to open the door. Her world shatters again as she realises that the happy hours she spent with Bill yesterday have been betrayed by the lock.

She breaks down and starts crying. She prays to Oyo, and to all the other ancestors at home. She closes her eyes and projects her thoughts to her shrine in Tokyo where she has prayed more times than she can remember. She prays for a number of things, but above all she prays that her mother and aunt be spared the knowledge of the humiliation she is experiencing.

Late in the afternoon she cleans the flat and cooks a simple meal. On their return, Ellen and Dolly seem quite cheerful and the mood is lifted further when Bill arrives with a number of newspapers. There are beautiful photographs of Ellen in her traditional kimono in front of some Ikebana arrangements. There is also a write-up about the young girl who is to offer classes in Ikebana.

Despite her unhappiness, Yoriko cannot help feeling proud of the young woman. She congratulates her with many well-chosen Japanese words of encouragement and endearment. Using Ellen as interpreter, she thanks Bill sincerely for all the newspapers he has given her that she will send to her mother and aunt.

Everybody in Japan will be very happy!

Bill fills their glasses with sparkling wine and they all drink to the success of the flower shop. Even Dolly clicks her glass against Yoriko's. Nobody mentions the lock on the outside of the front door.

Yoriko looks at Bill, the handsome man with the smile on his face, the glass in his hand, and the secret in his heart. He is a stranger, she realises. She thought she knew him from the letters he wrote to her. But her pride will not allow her to accept that she has made a mistake in her evaluation of him. She looks at Dolly and identifies her as the obvious reason for Bill's betrayal.

⁓

Later that night, when he is home in Parktown, Bill's wife, Mable, mentions that she has read about a new Ikebana shop in the city. She is convinced that it will be a success. Bill feels a thrill of excitement running through him. He gets a kick out of the fact that his wife will never be able to guess just how deeply he is involved in the shop.

He prides himself on the way he has handled his life. As

the construction manager of a large South African building consortium, he has come a long way from being a simple country boy. He is inordinately proud of the way he has kept his life with Dolly a secret from his wife. And on the other hand, he is grateful to Mable for running the kind of home where he can entertain business associates in the manner to which the English are accustomed.

His only problem is Yoriko. She can destroy his carefully constructed world if she speaks to the wrong people.

~

When the outside lock clicks into place for the second day in a row, a cloud of depression descends on Yoriko. She, an inarticulate stranger in this country, is trapped in a strange, hostile world. Why is this happening to her? What mistakes did she make that she is being punished for now? Surely she could not have been wrong in giving her heart to a high-class person, and an artist, like Bill? Surely she could not have misunderstood the meaning and the messages he had spelt out so clearly in those lyrical letters?

There can only be one answer: he is bewitched! This no-good woman he is living with must be a special favourite of the dark forces. With their help, she has complete power over

Bill. As long as he keeps living with her, and allows Tagenaga to stay with her, they will be powerless against the onslaught of evil. Of that Yoriko is convinced.

Then Yoriko hears the front door open, and Bill walks into the sitting room, as if in answer to her prayers. He gives her the smile of long ago, the smile of home and Tokyo and the Far East. Yoriko greets him and leads him to the settee, sees that he is comfortably seated, then hurries off to the bathroom where she wrings out a small hand towel in boiling hot water. She brings it to him in the sitting room and, with gentle soothing movements, drapes it across his brow and over his tired eyes. While he relaxes with a thankful groan under this tender Japanese care, she mixes him a drink with ice and places it on the table next to his chair.

Yoriko seats herself on the floor and tells him shyly, in stunted sentences, that she has become convinced he is held prisoner in the clutches of this no-good woman. She removes the towel from his face and hands him his drink.

Bill leans back, really amused at the earnest manner in which Yoriko pleads with him in her fractured English. She tells him that he must get a flat immediately, and that the three of them will move into that flat where she will be a mother to Ellen. He will not have to put a lock on the door, because a mother's love locks a woman into a home much more securely than any mechanical lock devised by man. Obviously she cannot understand the law of this land that declares her to be a servant. But in their own flat he will of course be the master and she will be his servant, no matter what the law says.

'Yoriko,' Bill says, framing her face with his hands. 'As I tried to explain to you previously, this is Ellen's chance to prove her worth to herself as well as to me. She is still young and already moving into the social circle of these very rich ladies. As you so rightly figured out, she has not had a very happy childhood. In this country where women have a lot of freedom, the flower shop will give her the opportunity to make a go of life on her own. Last night she told me she would like to live in her own flat. I think it is a wonderful idea. As far as I am concerned I cannot get married while my wife is still alive, and Ellen's mother costs me a lot of money to support. I am sorry you had an idea that you could move in here and live with me as husband and wife.'

Yoriko looks at Bill, the tears in her throat choking her, preventing her from uttering a sound. She has only understood a few words of what he has said, as he has spoken much too quickly. But she understands enough to realise that he never meant the things he had said to her in Japan many years ago. Not a word in any of his letters came from his heart! She had allowed him access to her body and soul, sacrificing her own integrity and traditions. She had renounced her future as an artist – this precious gift from her ancestor Oyo – believing him to be the master painter, whom she could serve. She feels deeply ashamed, remembering the prayers, her begging the gods to intercede on her behalf so that Bill might answer her letters! Her guilt is surely too great for her ever to be forgiven!

Frustration blazes into a sudden blinding anger, forming large fiery red shapes behind her closed eyelids. She feels a cry pushing outwards, stifling her brain in a soundless rage.

Bill notices the tears trickling through her closed eyelids, sees her struggle bravely to control her emotions, and says to himself, 'Christ, the poor little thing really loves me.' He bends forward, placing his arms around her when suddenly he feels her body go limp in a faint. He picks her up gently, carries her to the bedroom, and lays her down on top of the bed. He stands undecided for a while, looking down at the delicate Japanese woman.

He is overcome with a sexual desire for this woman who cares so much for him. He bends down and pulls down her underwear.

Yoriko awakes with Bill on top her. She is totally aghast. Could this really be happening? Has she really entered the realms of darkness? She hears herself screaming and instinctively bites him on the shoulder with every bit of strength she possesses. The pain is excruciating and Bill shoots up; he desperately tries to zip up his trousers. Yoriko jumps from the bed and grabs hold of a pair of scissors lying on the side table. She holds it out in front of her and screams in Japanese. In her eyes Bill recognises the fury of someone capable of killing him. He touches the bite mark and sees that there is blood on his fingers. He retreats to the door, not taking his eyes from her. Things have spiralled totally out of control; this tiny person scares him.

In the lounge, he draws the curtains and leaves the darkened room with rapid strides, bent on an urgent mission. As the front door closes behind him, the outer lock automatically clicks into place.

Bill takes the road to Soweto, the sprawling township where more than a million black people live mostly in dire poverty. He does not usually travel this road alone, as white people cannot easily enter the township unescorted.

He has a contact number that he can phone for making special arrangements. But this morning he is in a hurry. It is of the utmost importance that he speaks to his childhood friend, Boy. This is too urgent to wait for Boy to contact him.

Bill and his family had not seen or heard from Boy or Anna

after they had left the road camp those many years ago. But shortly after his arrival in Johannesburg, Bill had literally bumped into Boy in bustling Eloff Street. They recognised each other immediately and since then they had met quite often.

Boy had taken him to a 'white' shebeen in Soweto, which was considered relatively safe, and there they'd had beer and talked about old times.

Boy told Bill that he and Anna had walked almost all the way to Egoli – Johannesburg – where they had stayed with members of their Sotho tribe, who had taken pity on them. It was illegal for them to be living in town without passports. Their friends had advised them to go into the suburbs where Anna might be able to get a job as a housemaid.

Anna managed to find a job as a domestic worker. But because she did not have a pass, she was employed illegally. The mistress of the house warned her to be careful. Under the pass laws, black people had to have special permits to move from one district to another. Anna was one of thousands of women who did not have a pass, but who was taken in illegally by white people. The only condition her employer had was that if Anna was caught without her pass, she was not to utter a word about them. Her employers would be fined for employing her and Anna would be sent to jail.

Anna was grateful for the room, because now Boy also had a place to sleep. She was careful not to let the people of the house know that her son would sneak into her room at night. Boy also shared the food she received from the mistress of the house.

In time, the people Anna worked for realised that her son was also living on their premises, and so the master of the house employed Boy as a gardener. It did not take long before someone offered Boy money to take orders for dagga from the other garden boys who tended the beautiful suburban gardens.

Anna and Boy hid the money that they earned in a hole the two of them dug under the loose cement paving behind their backyard room.

Boy and Anna were both diligent workers and well liked by the people of the house. The old man even taught Boy how to drive.

When Anna heard that Boy's father had been killed in a tribal clash between Sothos and Xhosas, she had a new sense of urgency – she wanted her son to have a good life, and this he could only achieve if he worked for himself. She did not want him to be stuck in a back room with her. She encouraged Boy to start his own taxi business.

They counted the money they had saved and Boy asked

the master of the house to help him buy a second-hand Volkswagen Kombi. The old man graciously lent him the shortfall interest free.

When Bill bumped into his childhood friend, Boy was already an independent businessman unhampered by the burden of having to discriminate between legal and illegal dealings. Some of his clients were prostitutes, and Bill would often ask him to arrange a meeting with one of them.

Bill speeds along the highway against the late morning traffic flowing into the city. He has one thing on his mind. He has convinced himself that Yoriko is not the innocent little angel she pretends to be. She is a she-devil, a wild thing capable of murder. All these Eastern mannerisms are only a skilful way of hiding her true communistic instincts. He thinks back to the massage parlours he'd visited in Japan and decides that there is no difference between Yoriko and the Japanese prostitutes he'd enjoyed so much. They had too had their sweet little rituals, all just to mask their own lust.

Alone at the flat, Yoriko is trembling. She holds a carving knife in her hands and wishes Bill would return; she is overwhelmed by a desire to stab him with this knife.

When she hears someone fiddling with the key, she grips

the knife and runs to the front door, but it opens long before she reaches it. She stops in her tracks when she sees the huge black man smiling at her. She has never been this close to a person of colour.

She screams with fright as he catches hold of her wrists, saying, 'Man, baby! You need help!' He deftly removes the knife from her hand and pushes his way further into the flat, forcing her to retreat backwards. She stares at him, petrified, and tries to push past him, but the big man does not budge. He tells her not to worry. Bill has sent him as a peace offering to fetch her and take her to the park so that she can paint there and calm her nerves.

When she hears Bill's name, she becomes a bit calmer. She sits down and asks him to speak slowly. Boy tells her that he and Bill are great friends. He walks into the kitchen where she can hear him opening cupboard doors. When he returns, he has a white tablet in his hand and commands her to drink it.

'Why?' Yoriko asks. 'Because you are stressed and Bill is sorry. He said this would calm your nerves,' he answers.

The black man looks at her with such determination that she swallows the pill without further protest. She will pretend to go along with his plan to paint in the park, but when they get there, she will run away. She hurries to her room, picks up her basket of paper and paint, and walks to the front door.

When they get to the vehicle, he shows her that the word 'taxi' is written on its side. This makes her more comfortable and she can already feel the calming effect of the pill. She leans back against the seat, her eyelids droop, and soon she is fast asleep.

Boy starts whistling and increases speed as he snakes through the Johannesburg traffic. It does not take him long before he turns off in the direction of Soweto and reaches his destination. Bill is standing on the veranda of Boy's shebeen, smirking, a blanket over his arm. He pats Boy on the back.

'Nice work!' he says. 'How long did it take?' Boy shrugs his shoulders. 'As long as it took,' he answers, shaking his head from side to side.

'Well, never mind. See you sometime. And thanks!' Bill lifts Yoriko out of the car.

'No problem,' Boy replies, making a U-turn before driving off in a cloud of dust.

Bill carries Yoriko inside the shack and lies her down on a bed with dirty sheets. While he waits for the other men, he undresses her and gets on top of her.

Yoriko wakes up. It is already dark outside. She is aware of excruciating pain shooting up between her legs. And then she sees Bill sitting at a table drinking with four black men. But when he realises she is awake, he comes over.

'Did you enjoy it, baby? How about having something to drink?' He holds out a pill and a glass of water. She turns her head away, but he presses both her cheeks together with one hand, thus forcing open her lips and sticking the pill in her mouth. She feels groggy and parched, too weak to resist, and greedily takes a few sips of something that looks like watery porridge before the bitter taste makes her turn her head away in disgust.

When he picks her up, she feels the searing pain before she loses consciousness again.

When Bill walks into the flat later that evening with Yoriko wrapped in a blanket in his arms, both Dolly and Ellen are already in bed. He calls out to them that he is putting Yoriko on the settee as she is dead drunk. On his way out he sticks his head into the bedroom, telling them that they had better leave her to sleep off her drunken stupor in the morning, as one never knew how the skokiaan, a thick brew drunk by many township people, could affect her.

When Yoriko wakes up, the sun is streaming in through the windows. She groans with pain, her back aches, and her legs feel as though they have been torn out of their sockets. As the blanket falls away from her body she notices the bruises on her upper arms and a tremendous feeling of despondency overwhelms her.

She stumbles to the bathroom where she stands under the shower, washing and cleansing her body frenetically, as though trying to scrub away the outer layer of her skin. Her longing to be home is an indescribably intense physical pain, and she cries out helplessly. How does one rise above the utter degradation of such defilement? How can she face her mother and her aunt ever again? She has no doubt that her mother will understand, but with what sadness and sacrifice will this knowledge enshroud them!

Yoriko dresses in her pure silk kimono. The one she would have worn after the wedding. She places the shrine in the middle of the floor and with great difficulty sinks down onto her knees to pray. How angry Oyo and the other ancestors must be with her. She, who had been given a wonderful talent and who had qualified as a sumi-e artist, was never content. She had begged them to bring Bill back to her. She had begged them for the love of a man who was clearly not worthy.

In desperation, she throws the contents of her suitcase and her handbag onto the floor. She needs her things around her to anchor her in her desolation.

Then she sees the card with the name of the woman called Naka printed on it. It is the woman she had spoken to at the cultural centre years ago and who had promised to find out more about Bill once she was back in Johannesburg.

Perhaps this woman with the Samurai name, which means a leader with strong spiritual abilities, can help her. How can she make contact with her? During the day the telephone is locked and Dolly has the key. She is at a loss as to how to go about getting in touch with Naka. If only she could explain herself and her hopeless situation in her own language. Tonight she will pray and make a plan, she decides, and before tomorrow she will have thought of a way to attract attention.

Oyo be praised! Suddenly Yoriko is back in the world of the living! Of course Oyo will know the right thing to do. She bows deeply, her forehead touching the floor, thanking Oyo, and joy and happiness floods the colour back into her cheeks.

Yoriko picks up the shrine and places it on the mantelpiece. She moves as quickly as her aching body will allow. She begins to clean the flat and later she prepares the evening meal. When Dolly and Ellen arrive home, she greets them with a pleasant smile and many questions about their day at the flower shop. Ellen is even more excited than she had been yesterday. There had been many people in the shop and she'd had several inquiries about Ikebana lessons.

The next morning Yoriko is up early, having lain awake for most of the night perfecting her plan. She hurries out onto the balcony, leans over the parapet, and watches the people walking out of the building onto the street. She sees a man and she takes note of the colour of his suit and the way his black hair is combed over his head. After a while she has identified at least three people whom she is absolutely sure she will be able to recognise if she were to see them walking back into the building anytime today.

She stays on the balcony until Ellen calls, wanting to know what she is doing outside so early in the morning. Anxiously, Yoriko waits for Dolly and Ellen to leave the flat. This morning she welcomes the click of the lock. Still petrified that the black man might come and open the door of the flat again sometime today, she fastens the inside safety chain on the front door, and pushes a big wooden chest up against it.

Yoriko brings her painting basket to the kitchen table, takes out a few sheets of drawing paper, and cuts them up into small squares the size of her palm. On the one side of each square she paints the Japanese good luck sign, and on the other she writes, 'Help!' in red paint. Underneath that she writes the number of the flat and the floor number. Right at the bottom she signs her name the Japanese way.

She deftly folds some of the squares into origami baskets

into which she places squares of paper with her message on them. Then she pins each of the squares to an orange taken from the fruit bowl. She arranges them on the table on the balcony. Should Bill or anybody else come into the flat, they might be passed off as Japanese decorations!

She spends most of the morning on the balcony, waiting.

Just after noon a man appears walking along the street towards the entrance of the building. Is this the same squat little figure with the brown suit and black hair she had noticed earlier this morning? She is so nervous and excited that she can hardly breathe.

With trembling fingers she picks up one of the oranges with the little paper basket attached to it. How long will it take for this to drop onto the tarmac below? Her heart turns cold with fear, as suddenly she knows she should have dropped an orange from the balcony this morning to see how long it would take to reach the ground. Now there is not a second to lose. She must immediately drop the paper basket. Perhaps he might even look up and notice this white object falling from the sky.

She lets her wrist rest on the railing of the balcony before opening her fingers and letting the basket fall. Then she notices the little squares of paper fluttering down like confetti, blowing away in the breeze. The wind has torn the basket.

How stupid of her not to have thought of this before. She should have written the message in Indian ink on one of her white handkerchiefs! Tears blur her vision as she walks away from the balustrade, automatically picking up the other two paper baskets and removing the oranges. She walks into the flat, wondering how to rewrite the messages and think up a better way of attracting attention. Dejection has replaced the excitement she felt a few minutes ago. She flings herself down on the settee, burrowing her head in the cushions.

Faintly, somewhere in the distance, Yoriko hears a bell ringing. She lifts her head from the cushions. She hears the bell again, clearly, and realises it is at the door of this flat. A distinctive voice is calling urgently, 'Hello! Hello?'

She bursts into tears while relief floods her body. Through the locked door she tries her best to explain to the voice on the other side to contact Naka, and to tell her that the Japanese artist needs her help. Please. Yoriko passes a picture she has painted and Naka's business card through the gap left between the bottom of the door and the floor. The man asks her if he must break down the door, but Yoriko pleads with him only to phone Naka. At this stage she trusts nobody in this country and she feels safe behind the locked door. The man reassures her repeatedly that he is the right person to carry out her instructions, informing her he is a great admirer of art, and it gives him great pleasure to see such beautiful work.

After he has gone, Yoriko kneels down in front of the shrine to thank Oyo.

When the phone rings later that evening, Ellen rushes to answer it.

'Who? I am sorry, I did not catch the name?' She looks up, perplexed. 'Yoriko? You want to speak to Yoriko?'

She listens for a second and then asks suspiciously: 'What do you want to speak to her for? She can't understand much English. Can I interpret for you?' She looks at Yoriko, points a finger at the phone, and lifts an eyebrow. Then she continues with the conversation. 'What I'd like to know is, who are you, and where did you get this telephone number from?'

Yoriko watches Ellen keenly, seeing her listening with a slight smile on her face while nodding her head up and down. Then she looks up in surprise and says: 'Really? Then I suppose you had better say hello to her.'

Yoriko takes the phone and says, 'Yoriko, hyiaku.' She listens for a moment, then her eyes sparkle and she says excitedly, 'Greetings Naka! Sayonara! Naka come to Yoriko, soon? Tonight? Please?'

Ellen moans, speaking rapidly in Japanese. 'Oh, for Christ's sake, Yoriko! Are you out of your mind? We do not want visitors now. It is late and I want you to do my hair tonight.'

Yoriko looks at Ellen imploringly. 'Please. She wants to see Yoriko. Tell her address.'

Ellen takes the phone from Yoriko and says, 'It's much too late to come and visit tonight. Yes, I suppose tomorrow would be all right.' She gives the name and address of the building and the number of the flat, then puts down the receiver, gives Yoriko an enquiring look and demands curtly, 'Well, what was all that about?'

Calmly, she explains that it was Naka, an artist friend whom she had met overseas, and Naka wanted to see her urgently because she wants to discuss Asian painting with her.

She deftly changes the subject by asking Ellen what had happened at the flower shop earlier in the day. Ellen's face lights up as she begins to tell Yoriko about the posh women who had come to the shop.

After Ellen and Dolly have fallen asleep, Yoriko is still lying awake on her blankets on the floor. She is nervously apprehensive about meeting Naka. What if they find they cannot communicate at all?

When I put down the receiver of the telephone I am thoroughly bemused. I cannot believe the coincidence. Just last night, as I was working on an arts paper relating to Eastern arts, I was thinking of Yoriko and wishing that I could ask for some insight from her.

I have not heard from her all these years. Then today I get a phone call from a strange man who gave me this number. He only told me that he was asked to pass on a message, which he duly did.

When Tony arrives home from a meeting, I am exploding with excitement. He suggests that I take Yoriko with me the next day when I attend a conference on Eastern art.

The next morning, I decide to make a quick stop at the flat where Yoriko is staying. I want to make sure that there was no misunderstanding about picking her up later in the morning and taking her to the conference with me.

The door is opened by a young blonde girl in a kimono. I recognise her immediately from the photographs in the newspapers. There was a wonderful piece about the young Johannesburg girl who had studied Ikebana in Japan and had returned to open a shop in the affluent suburb of Rosebank. She is the very first South African girl to qualify in this Eastern art of flower arranging.

'I read all about you in the newspapers last night, and must congratulate you on your exceptional achievement,' I say to her. She seems shy and pleased at the same time. 'I am sorry, but my mother has already left for the shop,' she says.

'I am not looking for your mother, I am here to pick up Yoriko,' I say. She tells me that Yoriko is still busy preparing her breakfast, but she invites me into the kitchen.

'Hello!' I greet Yoriko with enthusiasm. 'It is a pleasure to meet you again after all these years. Welcome to our country.'

Yoriko is clearly pleased to see me. She smiles and bows low while telling me to take a seat.

I turn to Ellen to ask if Yoriko is helping her in the shop and with the Ikebana-lessons.

'Oh no!' Ellen replies. 'I can't allow that. It might be embarrassing to the ladies, considering where she comes from.'

'Surely not,' I laugh in disbelief. 'Those ladies have a sincere love and understanding of the Eastern arts, and would be honoured to meet your mentor. I read in the paper that you stayed with a Japanese family in Japan. I presume this was Yoriko's family?'

'Well, we wouldn't like to get into trouble. We do not want people to know that Yoriko is living here.'

I decide to ignore this and ask her: 'But now that she is here, taking her to see all the sights must be quite a pleasure for you?'

'Not really,' is the unexpected reply. 'It cost a lot of money to bring her out here, and as she doesn't speak much English, it makes it very difficult for us to drive her around. Besides, all of us are working during the day.'

I notice that Ellen is very much on the defensive, while Yoriko looks at both of us enquiringly. Perhaps Ellen and her family are genuinely at a loss as to what to do with her except leave her alone here all day long. To a highly cultured and educated person like Yoriko it must be an extremely unhappy state of affairs. No wonder she tried to contact me and arranged for me to come over immediately, I think.

Turning to Ellen, I say: 'You will be pleased to know that I do have time. I would love to take Yoriko with me and show her around the city and the museums. There is an art conference in town that she may enjoy attending. Afterwards, I could perhaps take her to a Chinese restaurant for dinner?'

'I'll see what she says,' Ellen says noncommittally. She turns to Yoriko and they talk at length in Japanese. Eventually Yoriko nods her head vigorously and looks at me expectantly.

'What time will you be here to fetch her?' Ellen asks.

'I will be here at a quarter to ten. If you will excuse me now, I have to hurry to make the necessary arrangements.'

Yoriko assures me that she has understood what I have said. I say a hasty goodbye and leave.

The door has scarcely closed when Ellen starts asking questions.

'You have never mentioned this woman to me before. How did she get to hear about you staying with us?'

'Naka is my friend,' Yoriko answers evasively.

'If she is coming to fetch you in two hours' time, I might as well stay here until she arrives, then she can drop me off at my flower shop and you can see the place as well. It is beautiful.' Ellen is clearly very preoccupied with her own interests. 'Dolly will see to the assistants and make sure that they have the flowers ready for me by the time I arrive. My first class starts just after eleven.'

~

In the slow-moving morning traffic I think about my encounter with Ellen and Yoriko. There is something incongruous about the situation. In Japan, Yoriko had an undeniably proud bearing and presence. This morning she seemed almost servile. The two impressions of her do not fit. How does Ellen fit into the picture? And where is Yoriko's famous South African artist-boyfriend Bill Bosch? By the time I reach the lecture hall, I still have not reached any satisfactory conclusions. I locate the secretary immediately, who greets me with a clear sense of relief.

'Naka! You are just the person I am looking for! One of the

speakers had to cancel her lecture on Contemporary Sculpture and Electronic Music. We were wondering if you would help us out of this predicament by filling in this slot with something on Eastern art.'

Quite overcome by this unexpected honour, I delightedly tell her of my timely meeting with Yoriko.

'I would be honoured to give the lecture after lunch and introduce her to the audience. Even though she does not speak English fluently, just having our members meet her would please both of us tremendously.'

I try to call Yoriko at the flat but the phone only rings in my ear. In desperation, I call the office of the newspaper which had printed the pictures and feature on Ellen. Luckily they are able to give me the telephone number of the shop in Rosebank.

A woman answers and I ask to speak to Ellen.

'I'm sorry, she will only be in later this morning. May I take a message?'

I explain that I have been unable to get hold of Yoriko on the phone at the flat, and I tell the lady that I want to postpone my appointment with Yoriko a few hours.

'I am so sorry about that,' the lady says sweetly. 'Yoriko already has an appointment for this afternoon. I will be going into town soon, and will deliver the message to Yoriko herself.'

I ask for her name and she tells me she is Ellen's mother and that they have made other arrangements for Yoriko for tomorrow. 'Phone me tonight and we can discuss the matter further when we are all home and we can check with Yoriko.'

I am very disappointed about this turn of events, but as it is already quite late, I have to rush to be in time for the first lecture.

Dolly, thoroughly perplexed, replaces the receiver of the telephone in the private office of the flower shop. 'Who in the name of hell could that be?' she asks aloud, then congratulates herself for the way in which she had stalled the caller. Bill would have to handle this problem tonight. She does not want any strangers poking their noses into her affairs.

She is glad that she had the foresight to unplug the telephone at the flat this morning. When she sees Ellen she will make it clear that Yoriko is not to receive any further phone calls.

At a quarter past ten, Yoriko and Ellen are still waiting for Naka to come and fetch them. Yoriko is dressed in her very special kimono – the one she had brought all the way from Japan as a wedding gown for a ceremony she now knows will never take place.

'Huh!' Ellen snorts derisively. 'Fine friends you've got! Let me tell you, she's Afrikaans, and they are the people who have passed all these laws against you. You just can't trust them! One look at you, and they make promises they never intend to keep. Not many people are as decent as we are, putting you up in our home, like one of us.'

Yoriko bows her head, utterly humiliated by this young girl making fun of her. Filled with sudden remorse, Ellen briefly pats Yoriko on the shoulder and tells her that she has to go as she is already late for her Ikebana class. Because she feels sorry for Yoriko, Ellen decides not to lock the door behind her when she leaves.

⁓

As I sit in the lecture hall, I find it difficult to concentrate on what the speaker says. The audience laughs and I glance up regretfully, aware that I have missed some salient point. I try to force myself to pick up loose sentences, but I truly have no idea what the speaker is saying. In my mind I only see the proud Yoriko as I saw her in the cultural centre in Japan. What happened to her?

Glancing at my watch I notice that it is half past twelve. As the lecture will not continue for much longer, I look around for the quickest way out. As we leave the hall, a friend asks me to join her group for lunch in the cafeteria. Assuming that I am nervous because of the fact that I have to present a paper later, I decide that a light lunch may settle my stomach and I accept the invitation. The uneasy feeling I have about Yoriko remains.

～

Alone in the flat, Yoriko is once again inconsolable. She has been humiliated thoroughly. She cannot bear the thought that her humiliation will bring dishonour to her family.

As if in a trance, she moves towards the shrine and walks to the mirror hanging above a small table in the entrance hall.

She had taken great care arranging her hair this morning and dressing in the silk kimono. She fetches the sharp knife she saw Dolly use to split a whole frozen chicken, and places it in front of the shrine.

She bows her head and prays to Oyo. The weight of her karma rests heavily on her conscience. Considering her filial obedience and the dedicated life she has lived, she feels justified in asking forgiveness for mortal sins, so as not to carry them with her into the valley of death.

'Being a person of great sensitivity, integrity, and honour, I trusted this man, who swore eternal love before making love to me. I lived for the day when we would be united again. I am a woman who is too weak to live further. Before all my ancestors, I swear that I will rather commit hara-kiri than submit myself further to a life of deceit.'

Yoriko holds the knife in both hands. To die would be a desirable release from the hell she is living in now. To plunge the knife into her bowels, to free her body and release her soul, would be ecstasy indeed. Proudly, she stands upright: highly cultured, refined, and completely alone in a strange land.

※

After lunch I find myself reading from my notes in front of an audience of artists and friends.

I digress a moment to interject a few phrases that are not on the paper in front of me. I have to blink my eyes as I imagine seeing Yoriko standing at the back of the hall dressed in a kimono. I feel disoriented and it takes me a while to find the correct sentences on the page.

'Another custom the artists from the East faithfully adhere to is called Fudezuka. It is common knowledge in the East that certain paintbrushes possess certain spiritual qualities, which can assist artists in their work. Some brushes allow the colour to blend easily, while other brushes allow the colour to flow freely. They venerate these brushes and when a brush is old and can no longer be used, the artist keeps it in a special box with all the other used brushes. No artist will insult the living spirit of a faithful brush by carelessly throwing it away.

'According to their custom an artist will, when the time is right, gather all his old paintbrushes together and place them reverently into a little wooden casket. The artist will painstakingly select a suitable tombstone and have an inscription and his name engraved on the stone, very much in the same manner as we would engrave appropriate words on the tombstone of a beloved pet: "Well done, good and faithful companion."

'The artist sends invitations to all his friends and fellow artists announcing the day and time of the Fudezuka – the name given to the ceremonial burial of the Faithful Paintbrushes. On the appointed day the procession will walk slowly, in single file, behind the master carrying the casket to the burial ground of the paintbrushes, where they will bury the casket reverently and stand with bowed heads while the master finally rolls the headstone into place on top of the grave.'

I rush through the notes and then leave the hall before anybody can reach me. I feel compelled to drive to the block of flats where Yoriko is staying. I cannot explain the urgency I feel.

When nobody opens the door to the ringing bell, I turn the handle. I cannot keep myself from screaming when the door opens.

Rushing forward, I catch Yoriko in my arms as the knife drops from her grasp. Gently, I lie her down on the carpet while I feel the tears streaming down my face. I call her name and murmur soothing words. I stroke the dark hair away from her pale face. Eventually I notice her eyelashes flutter, and lean forward anxiously, calling her name. She stares at me with stricken eyes.

I slip my arm under her head and cradle her to my bosom. We sit like this for a while, until the colour returns to her cheeks.

'I'm sorry! Please, Naka understand, Yoriko sad heart.'

I hold her close, wipe away her tears and tell her in my own language how much I care, how sad I am for her.

'Yoriko no face woman,' she murmurs while trying to get up. I help her into a chair, pick up the knife, and take it to the kitchen, where I get her a glass of water. Watching her sip the water I realise that she has to leave the flat immediately.

'Yoriko, I want you to listen very carefully. I am taking you home with me, and I want you to stay with us for as long as you like.'

Fear flares in her eyes as she answers quickly, 'No, no! Yoriko not go!'

'Believe me, Yoriko, you must realise this is a matter of life and death for me as well as for you. I cannot leave you here after having seen that knife in your hand!'

'Please, Yoriko explain ...'

'You can explain to me at home. I am not letting you stay in this flat a moment longer than I can help it, and we must hurry.' I notice the basket with her painting materials and pick it up. I walk into a bedroom and look around for her suitcase.

Still protesting and darting me suspicious glances over her shoulder, she packs a few articles of clothing. I pick up her basket of inks, and smile at her saying, 'Come on. We must go.'

Not knowing how much time we had left to ourselves, nor what I would do if Ellen or her mother were to walk in on us, I put my arm around her shoulders and speak to her earnestly. 'Yoriko, I am frightened for you. We can try to make sense of everything when we are safe in my home.' I take her by the hand and walk towards the door.

At home I introduce her to all the members of my extended family living together in a large house built in the Spanish style around an open courtyard. The rambling house is big enough for all the family relations and many friends to come and go as they wish.

In one corner of the courtyard there is a fish pond with blue and yellow water lilies. The doves sit around on the roof, resting for a moment before they fly down to bathe amongst the goldfishes. Yoriko is entranced. The three dogs and two cats frolic around her feet, greeting this visitor from the East as though she is one of us and it is their pleasure to make her feel at home.

I show her to her room in the corner of the courtyard, where she places her few belongings on the small table beside the bed. 'Tonight Yoriko phone Ellen, yes?'

'Yes, tonight you must phone those friends of yours and tell them that I want you to stay with us. Later you will try and tell me why you had that knife in your hand this afternoon.'

With a closed expression on her face, she says, 'Yes, Yoriko tell Naka perhaps tomorrow.'

Later Yoriko asks me to call Ellen, and when her mother answers the phone, I recognise the voice from this morning. I remind her that she had promised to give Yoriko my message. She says that she realised only on arriving home from the shop that the phone was not plugged into its socket. She explains that as they got too many calls from clients after hours they would sometimes unplug it. 'We plug it back in in the mornings, but we clearly forgot to do it today,' she says.

She tells me that her husband Bill had arranged for Yoriko to accompany Ellen as a chaperone on her journey back from Japan. The agreement was that she would work as a servant, but they have had nothing but trouble from her. Bill was not home but, she would ask him to phone me and we could decide what to do about Yoriko.

I pass the phone to Yoriko so that she can speak to Ellen. After a lengthy conversation, during which many different emotions cross her face, Yoriko puts down the receiver and looks at me with an expression of great sadness.

The next morning I go into the garden and pick a bloom off our prized protea bush. I put it down in front of Yoriko. She happily sets out her ink stick paint and brushes and becomes totally engrossed in her art. With deft strokes she soon replicates the intricate flower on the paper.

At lunchtime we go to the hall where the conference is being held, and Yoriko is fêted with due honours by all my friends and fellow artists.

The days pass by happily, and I patiently wait for Yoriko to open up to me of her own free will.

The evening meal is the one best liked in our house, because everybody who is home helps to prepare it. Sometimes one person will be the cook with the others helping, while at other times each person prepares a different dish. With Yoriko in the house, we decide to try our hands at preparing a Japanese meal. After the evening meal we linger at the table, drinking coffee and, because of Yoriko, green tea. Young and old take part in discussing everything that comes to mind. Afrikaans is our home language but for Yoriko's sake we speak English. Each of us tries in his or her own way to help Yoriko improve her skills in this language.

Yoriko and I discover that we have a bond beyond words. With a single glance we understand what the other is thinking or wants to say. This brings us closer spiritually. In order to get the full benefit of our mutual compatibility we buy two identical Japanese–English dictionaries. While Yoriko's English skills improve daily, I have to admit that my attempts at speaking Japanese do not progress beyond sounds I am sure are only produced in a Japanese nursery school.

I take her on a road trip to the Drakensberg mountain range and show her parts of our beautiful country. Two weeks pass without her mentioning either Ellen or Bill, and not a word is said about her suicide attempt. She seems so content and happy that I sometimes have difficulty reconciling this woman with the unhappy person I picked up off the floor in Hillbrow.

Eventually Bill Bosch phones. He immediately apologises on Yoriko's behalf for the inconvenience she is causing us.

His daughter has told him that Yoriko had taken advantage of our kindness by telling us some ridiculous sob story. He emphasises that she is just a silly little shop assistant whom he had met casually on a trip to Japan. She is adept at doing quick ink sketches for sale to tourists. However, after his daughter had completed her studies in Japan and because she was so young, he had offered Yoriko the job of companion to his daughter on her way back to South Africa. Obviously this had gone to her head and she had let her imagination run away with her. He would have contacted us sooner but he is the manager of a large construction firm and he was out of town. If she was giving us any trouble he would book her flight back to Japan right away.

I assure him that Yoriko can stay with us for as long as she likes, or until her visa expires.

'If that is what you want, let the decision be entirely your own responsibility,' he says.

I am sure he is smiling as he replaces the receiver, thinking how easy it was to get rid of her! A silly little shop assistant doing quick ink sketches for the tourists, indeed!

I walk across the courtyard to Yoriko's room to tell her that Bill Bosch had phoned. She almost jumps out of her chair on hearing this news. I am surprised by her reaction.

'Yoriko speak?' she asks.

Her response is unexpected. I did not realise that she would want to speak to him.

'Yoriko, I'm sorry. He did not say he wanted to speak to you.'

Her face becomes inscrutable.

'Naka phone Ellen, Yoriko speak Ellen, now. Yoriko say goodbye to Ellen. Yoriko also say goodbye to Bill Bosch.'

Luckily I have the numbers of the flat as well as the boutique. I try the boutique first and get Ellen on the line immediately. Yoriko takes the phone and as soon as she starts speaking in Japanese I hear the love in her voice. I realise that she must have been incredibly homesick these past few weeks. In spite of living in a house full of people, she must have longed for a chance to speak in her own language.

As she puts down the receiver, I put my arms around her and she bursts into tears. We walk to her room together where, for the first time since her arrival at my house, she opens up.

'Naka true heart and very good person. Now Yoriko speak everything.'

Hesitantly she starts telling me about the horrific experiences she had during her first week in South Africa. I listen with so much disbelief that at times I am sure I do not understand her correctly. I urge her to allow me to report what has happened to her to the police, but she cries and begs me not to. She wants to go home now, but she is too ashamed to face her family at home. All her relations are expecting letters to tell them of her wedding plans and they are looking forward to photographs. She now has nothing to show.

Later that day I have a brilliant plan to boost her morale. I contact a few newspapers. As I expected, they are keen to do a feature on this woman and her beautiful sumi-e paintings.

After the story appears in a number of newspapers, the owner of an art gallery contacts me. There is space for Yoriko to exhibit in her gallery for three weeks if she has enough paintings. Of course there are enough paintings thanks to her daily sessions while staying with us. The art crowd of Johannesburg flock to see Yoriko's work and every painting is sold.

The day before Yoriko's departure she tells me in detail exactly what procedure to follow when I take her to the airport.

We must stand and at the departure gate, and she will bow deeply out of respect for me. Oyo has chosen me as her pillar of strength because she is such a frail and sinful woman, given to impetuous thoughts and actions, she tells me. While she is still bowing from the waist down, I, as her mentor, should take my leave and walk away without a word. By the time she stands up straight again, I will have moved out of sight and into her heart. In this way I will give her the strength to travel back to her own people, her career as an artist and her happiness at home.

'And Bill?' I ask.

'Bill is dead,' she replies. I take this to mean that her love for him has died.

A month later I am surprised to receive a letter from Yoriko, written in her own hand and using the Roman alphabet! It must have taken her a long time to write this letter. It is a tremendous achievement for someone who could barely speak the language a month before. In the letter she tells me that she arrived safely in Japan and that she is thankful for my kindness. She writes that she has burnt all the photographs and letters Bill had sent her.

I receive a second letter two months later. Yoriko tells me that she frequently has bad nightmares during which she shouts out the word 'Kill!' This disturbs her greatly.

Shortly thereafter, her next letter tells me that she has received a cable from Ellen – Bill Bosch had died in an accident. Nobody could understand how his neck was broken as it was a minor accident without much damage to his vehicle.

However, I realise that Yoriko is not surprised by his death. She writes: 'Yoriko now understands bad dreams. I am understand his car accident because Oyo angry at him.'

As I fold the letter, I look up at the painting I have tacked to the wall. When I returned from the airport on the day Yoriko went back to Japan, I found it lying on the bed she had slept in. It is the little cameo Bill painted of Yoriko the day they had tea in the restaurant at the botanical gardens.

I am always remember ~~mounts~~ Dragonsberg in South Africa. With Naka. ~~an you~~ I saw Naka house to Marina beach your house drive car.
I will write publish book South Africa stay in your house and saw mount Dragonsbe-rg interesting story and ~~myself~~ orien-tal dragon. ~~painting~~. painting of of miracle story.
1989. Happy New year I will Painting of Bamboo with sparrow to again head of Country, and an Ambassador in Tokyo now I am got good boy friend. because He is same Spirit midium D.R. scholar. of cause He is single. never marriage. same age. myself. very famous Prof. ~~in Japan~~. of University. very kindly best heart man. but he is very very busy work. not free time. MR ABE 5 years ago bad ill. but now well. MR ABE know. my boy friend and pleased.

my boy friend always wrot magazine
and book about Reiko get miracle
story. always help my work Sumie.
now I am very dissapointed because
I can't ~~try~~ English letter.
I hope you are understand this
letter. now. I am very very busy.
maybe I will hold an Exhibition
at the Tokyo. now Paintings every
day.
I'm so sorry I can't letter always
to you but I never for get Naka
great heat and stay in your good
house.
I will write you again.
give my regards to your family

    lot of love

                         ▮ & mother

Happy New Year
1989.

Painted